Gratitude

Also by the Author

Not the Way It's Supposed to Be: A Breviary of Sin (1995)

*Beyond Doubt: Faith-Building Devotions
on Questions Christians Ask (2001)*

*Engaging God's World: A Christian Vision
of Faith, Learning, and Living (2002)*

*Reading for Preaching: The Preacher in Conversation
with Storytellers, Biographers, Poets, and Journalists (2013)*

Morning and Evening Prayers (2021)

*Under the Wings of God: Twenty Biblical
Reflections for a Deeper Faith (2023)*

Gratitude

Why Giving Thanks Is
the Key to Our Well-Being

CORNELIUS
PLANTINGA

BrazosPress
a division of Baker Publishing Group
Grand Rapids, Michigan

Published by Brazos Press
a division of Baker Publishing Group
Grand Rapids, Michigan
www.brazospress.com

Printed in the United States of America

Library of Congress Cataloging-in-Publication Data
Names: Plantinga, Cornelius, 1946– author.
Title: Gratitude : why giving thanks is the key to our well-being / Cornelius Plantinga
Description: Grand Rapids, Michigan : Brazos Press, a division of Baker Publishing
    Group, [2024] | Includes bibliographical references.
Identifiers: LCCN 2023028481 | ISBN 9781587436222 (cloth) | ISBN
    9781493444946 (ebook)
Subjects: LCSH: Gratitude—Religious aspects—Christianity.
Classification: LCC BV4647.G8 P53 2024 | DDC 179/.9—dc23/eng/20230814
LC record available at https://lccn.loc.gov/2023028481

The author is represented by and this book is published in association with the literary agency of BBH Literary, LLC, www.bbhliterary.com.

Baker Publishing Group publications use paper produced from sustainable forestry practices and post-consumer waste whenever possible.

24   25   26   27   28   29   30   7   6   5   4   3   2   1

For Nathan and Adam, two splendid sons

Contents

Introduction

It's one of the first courtesies little Noah learns. His mom hands him a cookie or a toy and asks, "What do you say?" Noah is slow on the uptake, so she follows up: "Say thank you, honey." And Noah obliges by mimicking his mom.

"Say please!" "Say thank you!" "Say sorry!" None of these courtesies is spontaneous for a child. All must be taught.

And mimicry isn't the only way to teach them. Maybe Noah's dad reads him a bedtime story titled *Bear Says Thanks*. In this story a fluffy, lovable bear wants to show his gratitude to each of his animal friends by laying out a feast for them. There's just one problem: his cupboards are bare. So his generous friends each bring a platter to pass, and Bear says "Thanks!" as they come through the door. When they sit to eat, Bear laments that he has no food of his own for the feast, but his friends pipe up that Bear has stories to share.

Little Noah is treated to a story of animal generosity and gratitude.

Noah will grow up into a world in which saying thank you is a social lubricant. We say and hear it twenty times a day. At the bank, in a store, on a plane—wherever small favors are given and received—we murmur our thanks. Doing so seems to make things go better and causes people to like each other more. The practice is so common we never notice it till someone omits it.

These are routine thanks that ease our way through daily life. But we sometimes experience weightier gratitude. Maybe my seventh-grade teacher comforts me after I've been bullied and then goes to straighten out the bully. Maybe my friend offers me a truly thoughtful gift, one they clearly had pondered for a while. Maybe my pastor or therapist counsels me in a way that changes my life. These are substantial favors, and we owe substantial thanks for them.

Above all else, there are the dynamic works of God. God is a mighty Creator whose love and imagination give us surging oceans, burbling streams, freshwater lakes with miles of sandy beach, and quiet ponds on which migrating geese ski to a stop.

God is also a determined Redeemer who rescues Israel from Egypt, provides for her in the wilderness, and delivers her to the promised land. In the New Testament, Scripture's recital of the mighty acts of God centers on the work of Jesus Christ and most especially on his death and resurrection. "He is the atoning sacrifice for our sins, and not for ours only but also for the sins of the whole world" (1 John 2:2). As the Apostles' Creed says, in him we have "the forgiveness of sins, the resurrection of the body, and the life everlasting." You might say that the whole Christian life is a way of trying, however inadequately, to give thanks for these magnificent gifts.

As a lifelong student of the Bible, I've noticed how often its writers thank God for such blessings and summon readers to join them. Some writers do this despite being up to their neck in trouble. They treat gratitude as an especially *urgent* necessity.

In the New Testament, we can catch a sense of their thankfulness by reflecting on the Greek word for it, *eucharistia*—from which we get the word "Eucharist." The Gospels tell us the story of Jesus's Last Supper with his friends and of how he blessed the bread and gave thanks for the cup: "This is my body." "This is my blood." The world's great *eucharistia*, its great thanksgiving, was transpiring before Jesus's disciples. With Christians all over the world, we rehearse it every time we celebrate the Lord's Supper. Most Christian liturgies for the Lord's Supper include the Great Thanksgiving or the Great Prayer of Thanksgiving.

Inspect the word *eucharistia* and you'll see that its center is the word *charis*, which means, remarkably, both "grace" and "gratitude."

This one little word says practically the whole of the Christian religion. Christianity is a religion of God's grace and our gratitude, centering on Jesus's brave sacrifice of his life.

Once we Christians become aware of the importance of gratitude, we start to see occasions for it everywhere. Look around. There is so much in life to give thanks for! Small things, medium things, colossal things. Post-it Notes, reliable cars, mountain peaks. You'll also see that the happiest human beings seem to be the most grateful. Why? Could it be that gratitude is an engine of joy? A *powerful* engine of joy?

Over the years, I've become interested in gratitude: what it is, how I get it, what keeps me from getting it, what happens to me if I have it. Joy happens to me. Contentment too. Maybe also generosity toward others. Wonderfully, if I have generosity and gratitude, my relationships warm up a lot. Psychologists in recent years have discovered that grateful people

3

have higher energy and lower blood pressure. They have less frustration and insomnia. They have more patience and hope. In fact, as we'll see in chapter 4, gratitude is *the single best predictor of human well-being.*

Is it OK to try for gratitude just to feel better?

Why does Scripture put such a premium on gratitude—urging it, commanding it, making a sacred duty out of it? Suppose I try to do my duty, but then I look around me at human and animal suffering. How can I seriously thank God when the world seems so awful?

Yet, amid awfulness, real goods persist. What's it like to savor and celebrate them? How might I keep a record of my thanks for them? How do I say my thanks, and to whom? What if some of the people who most helped me are currently dead?

If I am grateful for something, how do I take proper care of it? If the best way to say thanks is obedience to God and benevolence toward others, how do I tackle these assignments?

Finally, what's a sampling of the rich gifts that should trigger human thanks?

As I've thought about gratitude, one question has kept pricking my mind. In 1 Corinthians 4:7 Paul asks simply, "What do you have that you did not receive?" And the question makes me defensive. Haven't I worked hard for my success? Hasn't my effort achieved good things? How about my determination and sense of purpose?

But then I have to admit that the energy for my hard work came from God and the motive to do it from my parents and teachers. I'm not entirely sure where my determination and sense of purpose came from, but I'm pretty sure I didn't invent them.

So, what do I have that I did not receive?

What Is Gratitude?

The celebrated CBS newsmagazine *60 Minutes* presented a segment on August 14, 2022, titled "Hope Chicago." The segment tells a remarkable story about what happened to students at a high school on Chicago's South Side one day. On February 24, 2022, students at Johnson College Prep found themselves called into a school assembly without any idea why.[1]

Almost all the students at Johnson College Prep are African American. Many come from households with low incomes, and virtually all must dodge violence to get to school. Yet their high school is aptly named. These students hope to attend college. Fortunately, many JCP students are bright and qualified for college.

Their problem is money. Even with scholarships, many of the students can't afford to go to college. They can't bridge the gap between what their scholarship provides and what college costs. Besides, part of every scholarship package is likely to be a loan, which would saddle the students with intolerable debt.

So, as the students sat in assembly on that February day, they needed a miracle.

They got one. In fact, they got the shock of their lives. A millionaire businessman by the name of Pete Kadens walked on stage and greeted the students. Kadens is cofounder and former CEO of Green Thumb Industries, and he had a surprise for the students. He told them they would walk out of the assembly "forever changed." The reason, he said, was that he was going to pay for their college tuition, their room and board, and all their books and expenses. Gathering himself, Pete Kadens said, "You are going to college for free."

Joy erupted. Students leaped to their feet. They whistled and shouted and hugged and danced. Free! Could it be? Already overwhelmed, the students heard more. Pete Kadens was also providing a full-ride scholarship for a parent or guardian from each student's family!

CBS was there to record the event. One shell-shocked student, Kavarrion Newson, said that he had always trusted God to come through for him. Now, he said, you can bet that "God will get some special time from me tonight."

In the larger context of poverty in America, we might wish that *60 Minutes* had instead told of a successful crusade for justice in employment, wages, and housing in South Side Chicago. Then maybe the students at JCP wouldn't have needed Pete Kadens to swoop in with his miracle. Fair enough. But this thought cannot erase the plain fact that one winter day in Chicago, grateful high school students received news of a gift that would dramatically change their lives.

Gratitude, a Definition

After reading about the story of "Hope Chicago," do we even need a definition of gratitude? Maybe not, but here's an easy one: gratitude is whatever the students at Johnson College Prep experienced on February 24, 2022.

Let's add a more formal one: *gratitude is a glad sense of being gifted with something by someone and thus being indebted to the giver.* As we all know, this glad sense is often accompanied by at least a small rush of warm feeling toward the giver.

That's gratitude. It's a mixed sense of being blessed by and therefore indebted to a giver, usually accompanied by warm feelings toward that giver. Usually, but not always. If little Noah's mom tells him to say thank you, he might at some three-year-old level know that his mom just handed him a toy and be glad she did, but he might not feel any warmth toward her on that account.

Similarly, in a devout moment I might sincerely thank God for my good health—my thanks signaling that I know my health is a gift and that I owe God for it. I might feel an upsurge of warmth toward God—or not. (Maybe I just found out that a recent health scare was a false alarm.) The warmth is a welcome add-on. If I don't feel that warmth, I still have real gratitude.

Gratitude is not just a periodic sense of being blessed and indebted. Grateful people are inclined to feel gratitude most of the time. They have, so to speak, a light trigger for feeling like this. We could say they have a grateful *disposition*. If it remains stable over time, this disposition may be called a character trait. It's *in character* for a person with this trait to respond to good things with a sense of being blessed and indebted. Of course, we call a morally good character trait a virtue. Gratitude belongs in any list of splendid virtues—along with, say, compassion, kindness, patience, forgivingness, and generosity.

There's a big difference between occasionally feeling grateful and having a grateful disposition. In a seminar on gratitude at Calvin University in July 2017, psychologist Charlotte vanOyen-Witvliet explained to participants that people with a grateful disposition possess especially four tendencies:

- feeling grateful with higher *intensity* than others
- experiencing gratitude with greater *frequency*
- being grateful for a wider *array* of good things
- experiencing gratitude with greater *density*—that is, having a thicker group of people to whom they are grateful[2]

Philosopher Robert Roberts succinctly expresses the "framework" of what prompts gratitude: *a benefactor provides a benefit to a beneficiary*. Three B's. In this small drama, the beneficiary is aware of being blessed by and indebted to the benefactor for a benefit and so thanks the benefactor in some appropriate way.[3]

The Benefactor

You can't have classic gratitude without a giver. You have to thank *someone*. You can't sensibly thank "fate" or "evolution" or your "lucky stars" for your intelligence. An atheist can't rationally thank "the universe" or "Mother Nature" for a brilliant sunset. Thanking these entities makes no sense because none of these entities is personal. Needed rainfall isn't a gift if there is no giver. Atheists may enjoy and be enchanted by

In an episode of Charles Schulz's *Peanuts* comic strip, Charlie Brown's dog Snoopy writes a thank-you letter to his food bowl. "I think of you day and night," he says. "We have been through a lot together. . . . Thank you for being such a good pal to share a meal with."[a]

a full moon. They may be delighted or glad. But they are not thankful. They can't be because they have nobody to thank. When people try to thank fate or their lucky stars or Mother Nature for a gift, what they are doing is simply pretending for a moment that these things are personal. They personify them to make thanking them sound natural. And they borrow the language of gratitude to do it.[4]

In classic gratitude there is a real benefactor in the picture. For example, the person you love cooks a dinner you love. A traffic cop lets you off with a warning. Your boss offers you a thoughtful compliment on your work. These are clearly benefactors, and so you are grateful to them.

Often we know and can directly thank our benefactors. But sometimes we haven't a clue who they are. Who in my city first campaigned against real estate redlining, trying to open the door for racial minorities to get a mortgage? Who planned the beautiful bike paths that wind through my neck of the woods? Who were the national pioneers in making buildings accessible to people with disabilities?

I don't know, but that doesn't keep me from feeling that they have blessed me and others and that we are all indebted to them. If some of them are dead, that doesn't stop me. I just adapt my prayers a little: "Thank you, gracious God, for providing whoever did this." In fact, my gratitude will always

> "I have no idea to this day what those two Italian ladies were singin' about. . . . I like to think they were singin' about something so beautiful it can't be expressed in words, and makes your heart ache because of it. I tell you those voices soared, higher and farther than anybody in a gray place dares to dream. It was like some beautiful bird flapped into our drab little cage and made those walls dissolve away . . . and for the briefest of moments, every last man at Shawshank felt free."
>
> —Ellis Boyd "Red" Redding in *The Shawshank Redemption*[b]

have a double object, because God is the ultimate author of everything good. Thus, I want to thank my parents for nurturing me and thank God for providing them.

In the *60 Minutes* segment "Hope Chicago," students were deeply grateful to Pete Kadens for his generosity but also to God for inspiring him. That's why student Kavarrion Newson said that "God will get some special time from me tonight."

The Shawshank Redemption, a 1994 film drama written and directed by Frank Darabont, contains an unforgettable scene in which a benefactor blesses the inmates of Shawshank prison. In this scene, Tim Robbins's character Andy Dufresne, himself an inmate, enters the empty office of the prison warden and discovers a recording of Mozart's opera *The Marriage of Figaro*. He locks the door and plays a gorgeous duet from the opera on the prison PA system so all the inmates in the yard can hear it. They are caged, abused, and starved for beauty. They can't know for sure who is playing wondrous music for them, but they must be thinking it is God. Who else cares enough about them to fill them with joy?

The Benefit

As we know, gifts come in many forms. Andy Dufresne blessed his friends with unexpected music. Pete Kadens blessed the students at Johnson College Prep with scholarships. Abraham Lincoln blessed American slaves with the Emancipation Proclamation.

Christians in worship thank God for the good creation, for the grace of redemption, for life itself.

But most gifts are much less dramatic. Little Noah's mom hands him a cookie. A driver purposely slows down to let you slip into their lane. A teenager hugs their friend after a disappointing loss in volleyball.

Even smallish gifts may weigh more than we think. Suppose I am a guest for dinner in Evonne's home. At the table she hands me a platter of chicken with artichoke hearts, one of her signature dishes. I say thank you and that is that.

But if I ponder what is really going on here, my thanks will deepen. When Evonne hands me a plate of food, she's really saying, "Here, friend, take this. I want you to live. In fact, I want you to thrive." Handing food to a guest is momentous. It's almost sacramental.

The benefits may weigh more than we think. This is especially true if they cost the benefactor something. Pete Kadens's gift cost him millions—plus his serenity as teens all over the country started begging him to visit *their* school next. Andy Dufresne's gift infuriated the prison warden. Abraham Lincoln's gift made half his country hate him. But to beneficiaries, the cost of a benefit to the giver makes the gift even more precious.

Psychologist Solomon Schimmel suggests that a benefit is precious even if the benefactor tried to give it but failed.[5] I

11

think we understand. Some of the single moms of students at Johnson College Prep probably worked two jobs to try to send their kids to college but couldn't do it. I know of a man who heard news of a crisis and wanted to donate a goodly sum to relieve it. Because he lacked that sum, he tried to borrow it from a bank but was turned down. In both these cases the unsuccessful benefactors are still owed thanks.

The Beneficiary

My job as a beneficiary is simply to do a good job receiving benefactors' gifts and then thanking them.

What's involved in receiving a gift well?

As a good receiver I am fully aware that a benefit is an actual gift, that it came to me from outside myself. If I have intelligence, I didn't earn it. If God has blessed me from birth with a sunny disposition, I didn't achieve it. If I was raised in a loving home, I didn't construct it.

Second, as a good receiver I accept gifts graciously. If someone compliments me, I don't argue with them ("You say I'm smart, but you don't know the dumb thing I did just last week"). If a donor provides funds for a new building in town, I am grateful, not dismissive ("He just likes seeing his name on things"). If I am gathered with loved ones around a Christmas tree and you hand me your wrapped gift, I'll accept it with thanks. As I unwrap it, I'll protect the element of surprise you intended by wrapping it in the first place. I'll express surprise— real or faked.[6]

Third, as a good receiver I accept public works and services with appropriate thanks. Thus, I will express my thanks for citizenship in a free land by dutifully—even if not cheerfully—

The traditional *Book of Common Prayer* of the Church of England states in the Great Thanksgiving for Eucharist that we thank God because it is "meet"—that is, fitting and right and, in any case, our duty: "It is very meet, right, and our bounden duty, that we should at all times, and in all places, give thanks unto thee, O Lord, Holy Father, Almighty, Everlasting God, through Jesus Christ thine only Son our Lord."[c]

paying taxes. If people in the land are fighting voter suppression, I will support them. When I ponder the challenges facing elected representatives, I will pray for them.

Plenty of people focus on personal thanks for personal gifts but neglect to give thanks for the champions of public justice. I don't want to be one of those people.

Finally, as a good receiver I do not limit my thankfulness to the kind that erupts spontaneously. Of course, it does erupt that way sometimes, and it's wonderful when it does. But I will often thank benefactors simply because it's the right thing to do. It's the *appropriate* response to a gift. At the table of the Lord's Supper, the pastor leads us in the Great Prayer of Thanksgiving without first polling us to see how spontaneously thankful we feel.

Let me add something crucial. If it's right for me to thank someone who has given me something, then I am obliged to do it. Thanking someone for a gift is not just a social nicety; it's a moral duty.

But if it's my *duty* to say thank you for a gift, can I still be sincere in saying it? Of course. I may or may not have warm feelings toward you as I say thank you, but that's not the point. The point is that you gave me something and that I know it and acknowledge it. Would the biblical writers have urged us to give thanks if doing so was bound to be phony? Of course not. Dutiful thanks can be perfectly sincere.

Being Blessed

I said that gratitude is a mixed sense of being blessed and indebted. The recipient of a gift has been blessed by the giver and is now therefore indebted to them. I could have said "gifted" instead of "blessed" and been just as accurate. But I chose "blessed" because it suggests a gift coming from God. The suggestion is apt: God is the ultimate source of all good gifts.

John Calvin has a reputation in popular culture for being severe. But few theologians have been more exultant than Calvin over the magnificence and variety of God's blessings. God could have created the world with utilitarian aims, said Calvin, and provided humankind with mere necessities. But that's not who God is. What's remarkable is that the God of the universe wants not merely to support but also to delight us.

So God created towering trees, waving grasses, juicy fruits, and fragrant flowers.[7] Juicy fruits! Calvin was impressed with their sheer variety. Likely his idea was that, having been given apples, we could have done without oranges, mangoes, nectarines, peaches, and pears. But we don't have to do without them because God is the keeper of a whole orchard of delights. When it comes to baseball-sized fruit, we have quite a few to choose from.

Juicy fruits are from God, and we love them. But we may receive purely human gifts as blessings from God too. Kind deeds and encouraging words are goods. They assist us, and they adorn, enhance, and advance our lives. These gifts feel like blessings. They land in our lives with enough power to trigger our thanks. They help us not merely to live but also to flourish. The gifts seem credibly to come to us not just from another human but—higher up and further back—from God.

On July 2, 1964, President Lyndon B. Johnson signed into law the United States Civil Rights Act, thus legally prohibiting discrimination according to race, color, religion, sex, or national origin. It was later expanded by the Voting Rights Act of 1965. Inspired by the brave work of Martin Luther King Jr., this legislation was so novel and powerful and so obnoxious to racists that they have tried to chip away at it ever since. To the nation's Black citizens, long tyrannized and excluded, these laws were more than a gift. They were a blessing, an endowment by their Creator to enhance their life, liberty, and pursuit of happiness.

Being Indebted

People used to say thank you in a way that is now out of date. At one time, if you were hot and thirsty and I handed you a cup of cold water, you might have said, "Much obliged." It was a short way of saying, "You have given me a gift and now I am obligated to give you thanks in return."[8]

"Much obliged" is out of fashion, but we get the idea because people today still routinely speak of having incurred a "debt of gratitude." The basketball world owes James Naismith a debt of gratitude for having invented the game. Residents of Milwaukee who love its miles of public beaches on Lake Michigan owe the city's planners a debt of gratitude. People across the world owe the inventors of lifesaving vaccines a debt of gratitude.

This is a little striking because we usually think of debt as financial. You run up credit card debt. You get in deep trouble from gambling debt. You buy a house or a car and now have a loan debt. You live as a citizen of the United States and are affected in various unhappy ways by the trillions of dollars of national debt.

That's financial debt, and we are all acquainted with it. But, as philosopher Terrance McConnell points out, a debt of gratitude is different in significant ways. In a financial transaction, the provider *requires* payment. Not so with a debt of gratitude. If I hand you a cup of cold water, I don't demand your thanks. That would disqualify the water from being a gift. Moreover, if you are broke and your monthly rent is due, it would be fine if your cousin paid it. Not so with a debt of gratitude. If I hand *you* a cup of water, I expect *you*, and nobody else, to thank me. Finally, financial debts are repaid with something of equal value. Not so with a debt of gratitude.[9] Suppose out of sheer love your elderly grandmother knits you a woolen sweater. What she will expect back from you is enthusiastic thanks, not a knitted sweater of the same size and yarn.

People do us favors and give us gifts all the time. Many of them are small and our debt of gratitude may be satisfactorily paid by saying thank you. Some are larger and make us want to get a little more creative with our thanks. Some are so large they can never be fully repaid, so we pay our debt forward. Most children of terrific parents don't try to pay them back. They can't. But they can try to pay their debt forward by being terrific parents to their own children. If they succeed, it will be a mighty satisfactory outcome for everybody.

As for our debt of gratitude to God, I'll say a good deal about it in the next and succeeding chapters. It's enough for now to say that gratitude to God is preeminent among debts so large they can never be repaid.

2

How Do We Get Gratitude?

In the introduction I said that those of us with gratitude likely had parents who taught it to us when we were young. After handing us something good, one of our parents would prompt us: "What do you say?" "Can you say thank you?"

As we grew into the world, we heard thanks all around us and followed suit. We got in the habit. In families of believers, this habit has long included "saying grace" before meals, starting when we were kids. "God is great. God is good. Let us thank him for our food." Saying grace is a way of acknowledging that in so many ways we owe God for what's on our table.

Sad to say, a lot of folks are missing the gratitude piece of their lives. They didn't learn it when they were young, or they did but later forgot what they learned. In any case, gratitude is now a foreign language to them. All kinds of things block their gratitude, and in the next chapter we'll look at some.

For now, let's note that in synagogues and churches, believers practice gratitude as a regular part of worship. And they do it at a high level. They say thanks not just to a bakery clerk who saved four bran muffins for them but to God who saved their lives. In an assembly of believers, gratitude is not merely said but also chanted or sung—by children as well as adults and in groups ranging from families at Passover feasts to big congregations in megachurches. These are prime occasions for learning and practicing gratitude.

The Dayenu

For millennia Jews have celebrated Passover to commemorate God's rescue of their ancestors from slavery in Egypt. Passover begins with the Seder, a ritual feast. In its liturgy is the Dayenu, which means "it would have been enough." The liturgy names fifteen of God's mighty acts of rescue, and says of each Dayenu, "It would have been enough." If God had only rescued the Israelites from the Egyptians and not also given them the Egyptians' wealth, "Dayenu, it would have been enough."

> If He had given us their wealth and had not split the sea for us— Dayenu, it would have been enough!
>
> If He had split the sea for us and had not taken us through it on dry land—Dayenu, it would have been enough! . . .
>
> If He had brought us before Mount Sinai and had not given us the Torah—Dayenu, it would have been enough!
>
> If He had given us the Torah and had not brought us into the land of Israel—Dayenu, it would have been enough![1]

The Dayenu is a remarkable device. With its wonderful interior linkages, it piles up examples of God's generosity, celebrating each in turn, and thus piling up occasions for Israel's gratitude.[2]

"It would have been enough." That's gratitude speaking. Only gratitude "turns what we have into enough."[3]

The Mighty Acts of God

In reciting the mighty acts of God to trigger gratitude, the Dayenu follows clear biblical precedent. In Psalm 136, for example, God is not just a generic power; God is the Creator who made "the sun to rule over the day . . . the moon and stars to rule over the night." God is the exodus God who brought Israel out of Egypt "with a strong hand and an outstretched arm." God is the God of the promised land who "led his people through the wilderness" to reach it.

In each of the twenty-six verses of Psalm 136, the author recites a mighty deed of God and then leads worshipers in a chorus: "For his steadfast love endures forever." The point is that God's mighty acts in creation, redemption, and homecoming are never miscellaneous; they are always an explicit sign of God's steadfast love. It is God's love that prompts the psalmist to begin Psalm 136 very simply: "O give thanks to the LORD, for he is good."

The psalmist exclaims that the people of Israel do not have just any God; they have a good one!

Recounting God's mighty acts, expressing faith in God's goodness shown by those acts, and giving thanks for the whole works is classic biblical religion, Jewish and Christian alike. It centers itself solidly on creation, grace, and gratitude.

The Hebrew Bible tells of God's mighty acts in the creation, exodus, and delivery of Israel to the promised land. In the

"Because children have abounding vitality, because they are in spirit fierce and free, they therefore want things repeated and unchanged. They always say, 'Do it again,' and the grown-up person does it again until he is nearly dead. For grown-up people are not strong enough to exult in monotony. But perhaps God is strong enough to exult in monotony. It is possible that God says every morning, 'Do it again' to the sun; and every evening, 'Do it again' to the moon. . . . It may be that He has the eternal appetite of infancy; for we have sinned and grown old, and our Father is younger than we."

—G. K. Chesterton[a]

New Testament we find a notable shift in focus. Now we hear instead about God's mighty acts in Jesus Christ.

We find this story told most explicitly in the four Gospels. In them Jesus heals diseases, calms storms, casts out demons, serves miraculously multiplying food to great crowds, forgives sins committed against other people, and raises the dead.

God could have performed these mighty deeds by empowering a mere man to do them. But John, Paul, and the letter to the Hebrews combine to declare that Jesus Christ was no mere man but the eternally divine Son of God in the flesh. In fact, he is not just the Son of God; he is God the Son, worthy of not only praise but also worship.[4]

Testimony to God's mighty acts continues beyond the Gospels. The book of Acts tells of amazing miracles at Pentecost. There is the sound of a rushing wind, loud as a tornado. Miraculous fires settle on the disciples. They begin speaking in languages they have never learned. These things are amazing, but they are not the center of Pentecost. They are only attention-getters. They signal that the Holy Spirit is blowing in the room and that God is about to do something as big as the exodus. The center of Pentecost is that, as Peter preaches Jesus Christ to fellow Jews who are wearing the heavy armor of a corrupt generation, the Spirit of God cuts through their armor, pierces their heart, and saves them. This is a miracle as mighty as creation or the raising of the dead.

What exactly does Peter preach? He tells of Jesus's deeds of power, his signs and wonders, his death and resurrection. God is behind all of it, says Peter. God was acting in Christ (Acts 2:22–24). The mighty acts of Christ are the acts of God.

Faith in the Mighty Acts of God

Jews and Christians have long centered their faith on the mighty acts of God because these acts show God's goodness and especially God's love. God didn't have to create a world of creatures. God wasn't lonely. God didn't need a risky investment such as the human race. Not at all. Creation is an act of imaginative love. God graciously makes room in the universe for other sorts of beings, including us.

Creation is a mighty act of God. So is providence. God not only makes room in the universe for other sorts of beings but also provides for them there. Hence wheat fields and peach trees and sheepfolds. Hence God's acts of deliverance when God's people are in trouble. Hence the death and resurrection of Jesus, the mightiest act of all. What's more, these events are "for us," "for many," "for all" (Rom. 5:8, 15, 18). Jesus Christ wasn't just slain and raised. He was slain "for our trespasses and was raised for our justification"—that is, for our acceptance by God as free and forgiven people (4:25). Faith in God's mighty acts includes belief that they happened, of course. But

21

faith that they are "for us," "for many," "for all" moves us beyond belief to trust. As Paul writes, if God did not "spare his own Son, but gave him up for us all—how will he not also, along with him, graciously give us all things?" (8:32 NIV). All things!

Paul is talking about God's ultimate generosity and about our trust in it. Paul is *convinced* of all these marvelous things and especially of God's loving goodness that lies so unfailingly behind them:

> I am convinced that neither death, nor life, nor angels, nor rulers, nor things present, nor things to come, nor powers, nor height, nor depth, nor anything else in all creation, will be able to separate us from the love of God in Christ Jesus our Lord. (Rom. 8:38–39)

Only a numb Christian could absorb these words without a shiver along the spine. Here Christians want to wave banners and blow trumpets. Here the great apostle shakes his fist at the powers that threaten to undo us and shouts to them and to us and to the whole world, "If God is for us, who is against us?" (8:31).

If *God* is for us . . .

This kind of faith, says Robert Roberts, triggers *transcendent* gratitude.[5] Our gratitude for our health waxes and wanes along with our health itself. The same for our success and happiness. I ought to be grateful for my friend's gift, but if I'm in a cloudy mood with a chance of showers, I might not be. But gratitude for God's unfailing love, for God's mighty acts in Jesus Christ, for my membership in the people of God now and forever— this gratitude rises above my smaller sorts of gratitude because it focuses on the preeminent fact that nothing can ever separate me from "the love of God in Christ Jesus our Lord."

Observation and Reflection

For biblical believers, both Jews and Christians, gratitude arises from faith in God's goodness, shown by God's mighty acts in creation and redemption. For Christians these mighty acts center on Jesus Christ's death and resurrection. What's wonderful is that once I get in the habit of noting and celebrating God's goodness, I start to see it everywhere.

I said in the previous chapter that my gratitude for good things very often has a double object. If I watch a sunset, I have God alone to thank. But if my wife Kathleen says just the right word when I am discouraged, I'll want to thank both her and God—Kathleen for the encouraging word and God for making her the kind of person who would say it. If I learn the complex process by which my ear turns sound waves into an electrical signal that my brain translates into music, I will thank God alone, who imagined and created the process. But if my ears hear Johnny Cash singing "I Walk the Line," I will be grateful to both God and Johnny Cash.

And to others too if I am observant. In the case of Johnny Cash, a little research reveals a whole array of persons and influences that helped Cash compose his famous song and record it. Cash's mother taught him guitar as a boy. His first wife, Vivian Liberto, inspired Cash to write the song. Fellow artist Carl Perkins helped Cash with its title. Producer Sam Phillips helped him set its tempo. Bassist Marshall Grant and guitarist Luther Perkins accompanied Cash as he recorded the song.[6]

Reflecting on all this, I can't hear "I Walk the Line" without imagining Cash at the center of a whole web of helpers. But who arranged the web? How did Cash's mom happen to teach

C. S. Lewis lamented people who "would condemn as simply 'grey' the sky in which I am delightedly observing delicacies of pearl and dove and silver."[b]

him guitar and sing hymns with him as he grew up? Who was behind all the music-making in church when Cash was a boy? Who gave Johnny Cash his rich bass-baritone voice that any country music lover can identify after hearing only a few bars of it?

Grateful believers go through life alert, observant, mindful. They notice good things that only God could have produced, and they revel in their intricacies: A baby's listening ear that translates a mother's song into love. A setting sun that back-lights white cumulus clouds, turning them pewter. The taste of a fully ripened, field-grown tomato.

Observant believers also note a multitude of things that inspire their gratitude both to God and to other human beings. Suppose you are out in the world with your radar on. What might you notice?

- To protect an auto crash scene from traffic, a trucker angles his rig across the crash lane and sets out flares to warn oncoming motorists.
- A batter in a Little League game gets hit in the head by an errant pitch. The batter notices how bad the pitcher feels about it and trots out to the mound to hug him.
- Online reports of a natural disaster tell of volunteers who travel hundreds of miles to help people they do not know.

You observe such things and you are filled with thanks to the people who show such grace and also to God who inspires it. Maybe, like me, your radar picks up examples of grace not only from real life but also from fiction, where your gratitude goes out to the author who imagined and wrote them.

Author Ernest Hemingway purposely built a macho image for himself and was often nasty and sometimes cruel. But in his short story "The Capital of the World," Hemingway imagines a joke that is in fact a scene as gracious as any I know. Writer Ken Bazyn tells us about it:

> It seems that a remorseful father placed a personal ad in the newspaper *El Liberal*, which read: "PACO MEET ME AT HOTEL MONTANA NOON TUESDAY ALL IS FORGIVEN PAPA." What the father had forgotten is that Paco (short for Francisco) is a popular name. The Madrid Civil Guard had to be called to the Hotel Montana, because 800 Pacos had answered the ad.[7]

So far, we've seen that we get gratitude from being taught it and from living in an environment in which gratitude is routinely modeled. Beyond this, believers develop a transcendent form of gratitude by reflecting on God's goodness shown in God's mighty acts. We express and deepen such gratitude in worship, beginning when we are children. Once we believers have gotten in the habit of being grateful, we find triggers for gratitude everywhere. All we need to do is to move through God's world in an observant frame of mind.

In a perceptive article, David G. Allan asks a simple question:

> Which of these do you have going for you right now? Family. Friends. Love. Health. Freedom from war and natural disaster. Imagination. Community. A roof over our heads. Common decency. Hope.

Opportunity. Memories. Financial stability. Favorite places. Days off work. Good weather. The golden age of television. Books. Music. Ice cream. Weekends. A friendly exchange. Something good that happened today. Something bad that didn't happen today. A good cup of coffee.[8]

You could add your own: sports, your dog, your cat, good local government, your favorite sweater, maple trees outside your window . . .

Cultivating Gratitude

But what if, in the midst of all these good things, my gratitude is still sluggish? Fortunately, I'm not helpless. I can awaken my gratitude with time-tested strategies. Some of these will be familiar to you because you are practicing them right now. Others may be new. Have a look.

Journaling or keeping a list. Many people finish their day by jotting down what triggered gratitude, and some pray over their list. It's a way of being purposely attentive to the good things that come to us. Robert Emmons suggests that if we record these things very specifically and dwell on them, they start to magnify in our minds till they are almost splendid.[9] Moreover, if I keep my list according to the calendar, I can go back a year and see what blessings have persisted from then till now. That is an additional cause for gratitude. Journaling is helpful not just in recalling past sources of gratitude but also in getting us in the frame of mind for noticing new ones. And it needn't take the form of words alone. Some folks keep a photo album of things that excite their gratitude. I have a niece who posts such photos on Facebook to share with friends.

Testifying to what excites our thanks. Thanksgiving dinner is a prime occasion for people around the table to say what makes them grateful. Some families or groups of friends do this every time they meet for a meal. Like many others, my younger son's family engages in the "roses, thorns, and buds" exercise at the evening meal. Each family member tells of a "rose" in their life that day—something positive—and of a "thorn"—something negative—and of a "bud"—something with the potential to be positive. The roses and buds are often occasions for gratitude.

Keeping a happiness jar. Sound hokey? Maybe, but it works. It's really just another form of journaling. At the end of the day you write a note of gratitude for something or someone. Maybe someone cooked you a meal or texted their love or gave you good advice. It could be someone in the news. Maybe a country puts up signs on its border welcoming refugees. Maybe a national leader fulfills a pledge to reach across the aisle in genuine bipartisanship. Whatever it is, you write it up and drop it in the jar. Then, if you are slumping on some rainy Monday morning, you reach into your jar and pull out a note that picks you up. Some people are so devoted to their happiness jars that they decorate them.[10]

Apprenticing ourselves to grateful people. Every church has such people. Most families have them. Groups of friends have them too. We can watch grateful people. See what excites their gratitude. See what excites their gratitude even in the middle of trouble. We can observe them, imitate them, learn from them.

Arguing with ourselves. If we notice ingratitude in ourselves, we don't have to just sit with it. We can argue ourselves out of it.[11] Suppose I'm a partner in a business firm and hold my own just fine. But I'm not the star of the team. The star is a fabulously gifted woman who attracts the best clients, serves them in winning ways, and makes great profits for the firm and a great salary for herself. What if I resent her? And what if my resentment is just noticeable enough to contaminate team morale? I should take myself aside and say, "You numbskull! She's making you money! You ought to be grateful she's on *your* team and not with some rival firm—which is where she'll be if you keep acting like such a dimwit."

Pretending we are grateful till we are. In a chapter of *Mere Christianity* he called "Let's Pretend," C. S. Lewis remarks on a simple experience we have all had. If I ought to be friendly toward someone but don't feel friendly, I can act much more friendly than I feel, and I will find that in a few minutes my feelings get friendlier. This is "good hypocrisy," and it works beautifully with gratitude.[12]

Suppose my child surprises me with a party. I am the sort of private person who doesn't like surprise parties and doesn't want them. I thought I had made this clear to my child—but apparently not. Now, after the party, I know I have to thank my child for an event I hadn't wanted. I have to write her a thank-you note and express gratitude I don't have. As I write, I can't help thinking of the efforts she spent on my behalf: whom she called, what she purchased, what joy she took in hiding from me the upcoming surprise. And sure enough, I start to get the sense of being blessed by her and of owing her a debt of gratitude. I find warm feelings toward her arising in me like a favorable breeze.

Praying for gratitude. Nobody knows how petitionary prayer works, and sometimes it doesn't seem to work at all. Yet we do it because Jesus did it and taught us to do it. It's a basic part of following Jesus. In the strange and blessed chemistry of prayer to God, we often find that if we simply ask God for gratitude, it arrives. And strange things happen. Even if, after prayer, gratitude for a difficult loved one remains elusive, somehow the sheer fact of asking God for gratitude makes us deeply aware of—and thankful for—God's presence. God's presence with us is persistent, uncanny, and often realized through prayer.

Imagining Jesus at the Last Supper. Even before Gethsemane and Golgotha, Jesus suffered more than most of us will in our lifetime. He suffered more on the cross than all of us because he was absorbing into himself the sins of the whole world. He had some idea beforehand of what this would be like, and so he prayed to be spared it. And yet "on the night when he was betrayed [he] took a loaf of bread, and when he had given thanks, he broke it and said, 'This is my body that is for you'" (1 Cor. 11:23–24). Giving thanks for bread *under these circumstances.* "This is my body that is for you." Our minds can't grasp what is happening here. Only our hearts can hold it.

How do we get gratitude? I've tried to suggest as many ways as I can think of. No doubt there are others. But in the end, I have to say they are not enough. Besides my efforts, I'm going to need God's grace to soften my hard heart. Even as a child I had to be taught gratitude. It didn't come naturally. It still doesn't. I need the gracious power of the Holy Spirit to work in my heart and inspire my thanks.

All Christian virtues are both God's gift and our calling. The interplay between these things—between what God does and what we do in acquiring a virtue like gratitude—is a matter of great mystery. I'm confident we'll not be able to penetrate this mystery anytime soon, and I am equally confident that there is no need to do so.

3

What Blocks My Gratitude?

In 180 nations around the world, two million members of Alcoholics Anonymous meet regularly to help each other stay sober. They belong to well over a hundred thousand groups meeting in countries from Argentina to Ghana, from Germany to Japan, from Australia to the United States. In many places, including the US, meetings typically begin with a group recitation of the Serenity Prayer:

> God, grant me the serenity to accept the things I cannot change, the courage to change the things I can, and the wisdom to know the difference.[1]

Someone will then read the famous Twelve Steps from the so-called Big Book,[2] and—after several other preliminaries—the group will settle on a topic for the meeting. It might be one of the Twelve Steps, or it might be, say, patience or fear of relapsing or the role of sponsors. Members then offer reflection on the chosen topic. Before speaking, members introduce themselves by first name only—"I'm George, an alcoholic"—and the group responds, "Hi George!"

What George likely says next is "I'm grateful to God and to AA for this day of sobriety." Gratitude is a huge theme in AA meetings. Often it is itself the topic of the meeting. Members sometimes say that before they joined AA, they had little experience of gratitude. They had fought with family members and thus resented them. They had been apathetic about their job and so had lost it. They had been full of a self-loathing that crowded out anything close to gratitude. In other words, their alcoholism had blocked their gratitude.

Innocent Ingratitude

In the previous chapter we saw that we can get gratitude in lots of ways—from fostering faith in God's goodness to journaling, arguing with ourselves, and pretending we have gratitude till we do, among other means. While there are lots of ways to get gratitude, there are, sad to say, also lots of ways to block it.

Some of these are innocent. People with clinical anxiety or depression or shame disorder may be too troubled to experience gratitude. Those of us who know these troubles personally or who love someone with them will have a common testimony. Commands, even biblical commands, to be grateful are irrelevant and even offensive when directed at the anxious, depressed, or shamed person. Maybe they can barely get out of bed. How are they going to answer the call to be grateful? The same goes for people with alcoholism, cancer, or other forms of suffering so overwhelming that gratitude is, at the present, hard to come by.

Sometimes our gratitude gets stymied not by our own suffering but by the attitude of the giver. Maybe the giver wants to bend me to their will through their gift. Suppose my boss promotes me and then lets me know that by accepting the promotion I am swearing unquestioning loyalty to their agenda. I am unlikely to feel grateful for this gift that comes with such strings attached. My boss has blocked my gratitude.

Or suppose one of my friends has substantial wealth and loves to show it off. If I have reason to think their fancy gifts come from this love instead of from love for me, I won't be able to work up much gratitude for them.

Less Innocent Blocks

So maybe the person who gives me something is a known control freak or show-off. I have reason to suspect their motives. But what if I suspect *everybody's* motives? What if I cynically think "nobody is that good" when it comes to any act of generosity whatsoever?

Cynicism blocks gratitude. The skeptic looks at most things through narrowed eyes. The cynic is a skeptic who looks especially at people's *motives* that way. If I'm a cynic, I can't receive a gift—no matter how good-hearted the giver—without thinking, "What's the *real* reason I'm getting this?"

As a cynic, I think gratitude for gifts is naive and I believe that the thankful person is merely gullible. Thankful people may think givers have pure motives, but I know better. I'm nobody's fool. I've been around the block. I know everybody's got an angle.

Why are cynics so cynical? What makes them distrust the motives of somebody who has been kind to them? Maybe the cynic is proud of being nobody's fool. But maybe the cynic possesses not a towering ego but a fragile one. Or both. In any case, if I'm a cynic with a fragile ego, I may be aware that others are lauded for being generous and that I'm not. I say to myself, "OK, so I'm not generous—but neither is anybody else. If others get praised for being generous it's only because they've pulled the wool over people's eyes. I don't have to feel inferior. They're no better than I am."

Cynicism, like most twisted attitudes, is a real curse. The cynic blocks not only their own gratitude but also much else, including trust and love. If I can't trust the motives of my fellow workers, how can I collaborate with them? If I can't trust the motives of the person who says they love me, how can I love them back?

Self-sufficiency blocks gratitude. I may think I don't need good things from anybody else because I can take care of myself just fine. Such an attitude has its appeal: we all tend to approve when people support themselves financially. Leeching in-laws are not our favorites, and nobody wants their daughter to marry a guy who will become one. We like it when people pay as they go, and we want to conduct life this way ourselves.

But this makes receiving a gift a little awkward. We didn't pay for it. We have no right to it. Yet here it is, dropped in our lap by a gracious loved one, and now gratitude requires us to feel obliged or beholden. We may not like feeling that way. If I am obliged or beholden, doesn't that make me dependent? And isn't being dependent a subpar way to live in a proud country like the United States of America?

Self-sufficiency. Independence. Rugged individualism. Aversion to handouts. Where these attitudes reign, gratitude becomes uphill work.

Scott Hoezee observes that dependence in the US usually comes with a stigma attached. Who wants to be codependent or welfare dependent? What church member relishes a chance to depend on their deacons? What American patriot in the eighteenth century would have issued a Declaration of Dependence and hoped to stir the blood of patriots?[a]

When President Lyndon Johnson was a young teen in the hill country of Texas, his father Sam lost the family farm owing to unfavorable weather and had to move his family into a small house in town. The Johnsons had been an economic force in the hill country for generations, rich enough to have a luxury car and a chauffeur. Now they were poor and needed food handouts from neighbors to survive. Young Lyndon Johnson was not grateful for these handouts. He was ashamed of them and of being poor and of being mocked for being poor, and he spent the rest of his life trying to bury his teenage shame under a mound of achievement.[3]

Economic self-sufficiency is a usual goal for most of us and entirely understandable. But, apart from finances, the desire for self-sufficiency is isolating. If I can't graciously receive a well-meant gift from a friend, I imperil the friendship. If I shun the graciousness of my family—fearing that I will feel indebted to them for it—I successfully block gratitude as well as any sense of real fellowship or love. Most notably, if I can't accept my dependence on God for the gift of everything good in my life, I sabotage my most important relationship. I'm like a lung patient who resents their need for a resuscitator and so pulls the plug on it.

Greed blocks gratitude because it makes me discontent. If I'm never satisfied and always want more, I'm unlikely to be grateful for what I already have. This is a real disadvantage, to put it mildly.

Why? Because, as we've already seen, gratitude makes what we have enough. With greed there is never enough. I see ads telling me what I lack, and I solemnly believe them. I eye my neighbor's car and lose joy in my own. I earn a fine salary at work but resent that it's not the top salary.

On the other hand, if my desires are modest, I'm no longer so restless. I'm free to appreciate small events and simple things. Maybe I'm cooled by a refreshing breeze. Maybe my loved one says a particularly kind word. Maybe I am delighted by music I've never heard before. These simple things give me joy just because I am so grateful for them. And I can be grateful for them just because I am content with them. My soul is calm.

When I was a boy, my dad would walk me past the windows of downtown department and sporting goods stores and say to me, "Son, look at all these terrific things we can do without! We have so much already that we don't need them. Isn't that wonderful?"

My dad was teaching me gratitude: "We have so much." And he was teaching me contentment: "We don't need these terrific things." He knew that if I became grateful I would also be content. And he knew that gratitude and contentment are classic ingredients in human flourishing.

Greed makes us discontent. And it's contagious. It spreads through whole swaths of society in which people think it's normal to try hard to be super rich. Their appetite for riches consumes and coarsens them. They lose interest in small joys. Why wouldn't they? Small joys can't feed the ravenous beast in their soul. They are constantly aware that in their neck of the woods money is how you keep score. "Successful" as in "he's a successful man" comes to mean exclusively "he's a *financially* successful man." The results of life in this lane are discouraging, not the least because gratitude is so scarce there.

I want to be clear: the obstacle to gratitude I'm discussing here is not riches but *greed* for riches. All by itself, wealth may be a blessing or a curse depending on what we do with it; but greed is always a curse when it thwarts contentment and gratitude.

Apathy blocks gratitude. In the early centuries after Christ, desert monks gave a lot of thought to the sins that bedevil Christians, including themselves. Are there some sins that are particularly destructive? Are there *root* sins that cause other sins to grow out of them? After pondering this question, the monks drew up a list that became standard by the seventh century and has come down the ages as the seven deadly sins. Here they are: pride, envy, anger, sloth, greed, gluttony, and lust.

Greed almost surely played some role in the US financial meltdown of 2008. "So many people were in on it: people who had no business buying a home, with nothing down and nothing to pay for two years; people who had no business pushing such mortgages, but made fortunes doing so; people who had no business bundling those loans into securities and selling them to third parties, as if they were AAA bonds, but made fortunes doing so; people who had no business rating those loans as AAA, but made fortunes doing so; and people who had no business buying those bonds and putting them on their balance sheets so they could earn a little better yield, but made fortunes doing so."

—Thomas L. Friedman[b]

For centuries, preachers have warned against these sins. Priests have challenged penitents to confess them. Famous authors and artists have depicted them. All along, the sins were called "deadly" because, being so generative of other sins, they could destroy a person's life.

We've just discussed greed, and below we'll look at pride and envy. For now, consider sloth. We're tempted to think of it as laziness, and, when we do, the Bible's proverbs come to mind with their warnings against being a sluggard, a slacker, a lazybones. Probably the most famous of these warnings is phrased as a piece of blunt advice: "Go to the ant, you sluggard; consider its ways and be wise!" (Prov. 6:6 NIV).

But in the church's traditional treatment of the seven deadly sins, sloth is worse than mere laziness. It's utter boredom in the face of God's gifts. It's spiritual indifference or apathy. In effect, the slothful person says to God, "You are not interesting, and neither are your gifts." And the slothful person feels the same about friends, family, and the rest of humanity. None of them and none of their gifts are worth thinking about.

In a much-quoted passage, the British mystery writer Dorothy L. Sayers describes the slothful person as someone who

> believes in nothing, cares for nothing, seeks to know nothing, interferes with nothing, enjoys nothing, loves nothing, hates nothing, finds purpose in nothing, lives for nothing, and only remains alive because there is nothing he would die for.[4]

This sounds like it could be someone with severe clinical depression, and sloth can definitely be one of its symptoms. But indifference to the gifts of God and of others can also beset those of us without that diagnosis. I've long wondered about churches with short prayers, easy sermons, entertaining

"Sluggards do not plow in season; so at harvest time they look but find nothing."

—Proverbs 20:4 (NIV)^c

worship centered on earthly things. Is God not interesting to them? Are the gifts of God not worth celebrating at a little length?

That's indifference to God. What about my indifference to the gifts others bring to my life? Why don't I make something of them? Why can't I bestir myself about them? Why do I sometimes miss them altogether?

Apathy may be a defense mechanism, as some psychologists say. Maybe if my life hasn't turned out as I had hoped, I adopt an attitude that says I don't really care. Maybe. But there's no doubt about what apathy does to gratitude. It closes the door.

Resentment blocks gratitude. Resentment may be justifiable or not. In either case it will prevent gratitude. For a case of justifiable resentment, take an example close to home. Suppose your spouse consistently shuts you out, ignoring your opinions, your hopes, your very presence. You understandably resent this. After all, shouldn't spouses take a lively interest in each other? Maybe your spouse does have a few redeeming qualities. Maybe they are peaceable or well-groomed. But these agreeable traits aren't strong enough to offset what's wrong. You can't be grateful for your spouse, because being ignored in a marriage is a deal-breaker.

I may be justified in resenting that my spouse ignores me. But what if I miss work a lot and resent my boss for questioning me about it? What if I resent an *imagined* insult? What if I don't merely disagree with someone of a different political persuasion but also resent and hate them?[5] What if I come in second in a race and display "silver-medal syndrome"?[6] Predictably, such unjustified resentments stop anything close to gratitude for the persons I resent.

While we're thinking of silver-medal syndrome, we should look more closely at the kind of resentment it embodies. I have envy in mind, a specialized resentment that homes in on another person's advantage. The envier resents that others are smarter, richer, or more blessed in some other way. Maybe the envier is Cain, who resents that God seems more pleased with his brother Abel (Gen. 4:3–8). Or Saul, who resents that David is more popular than he is (1 Sam. 18:7–9). Or Salieri in the film *Amadeus*, who bitterly resents Mozart's sublime musical talent. Salieri is a so-so composer who had begged God for musical talent superior enough to make him God's voice to the world. God's response was instead to place supreme talent in Mozart, a brat who prances and giggles and talks dirty backward. Salieri's curse is that he is just gifted enough to see exactly how much Mozart's gift dwarfs his own.[7]

Cain, Saul, and Salieri resent a rival's advantage. But some folks seem to resent almost everything. Very little pleases them. Nothing satisfies them. Occasionally they manage a tight smile or a semi-pleasant word, but it looks forced. Their default mode is bellyaching. In their view, the country is full of losers. The church is full of hypocrites. Their critics are full of—well, you know. They're like the mythical farmer who had six chicks hatch and griped that all of them had died on him but five.

A sense of entitlement blocks gratitude. This is the big one. If the other blocks are barriers, entitlement is a wall. Think about it. If I am so special that life *owes* me its good things, what is there to be grateful about? If life owes me, nothing is a gift.

Entitlement is a classic form of the deadly sin of pride. Yes, there are righteous forms of pride. We all want goods and services from people who take pride in their work. If we have children, we hope they will grow up in ways we can be proud of.

But sinful pride is something else altogether. It's usually narcissistic—that is, self-absorbed, self-centered. And it's always conceited. A conceited person overestimates their stature in the world. They think their great stature warrants special treatment. Life owes them what they want because they deserve it. To them, this is simply the natural order of things, and nobody should interfere with it.

If we look around town, we can see this sense of entitlement at work everywhere.

- A preacher makes ignorant claims from the pulpit and expects to be believed because they presume to speak for God.
- You make a timely reply to a text or an email, and it becomes clear that the recipient feels slighted. They had felt entitled to an immediate reply.
- A restaurant accepts reservations only for parties of seven or more but receives a message from a diner who states that they are an exception: "I am a haute couture fashion designer with an ultra luxury collection. Unfortunately I'll only be able to come with 2–4

people, but I can't wait in line especially if on a business dinner or a date."[8]

- *BuzzFeed* asked the teachers among its readership for stories of entitled parents. Here's one: "Elementary art teacher here. I had a mom of a kindergartner write a curt email about how her daughter got paint on her shirt and that she'd send it back with her daughter the next day for me to clean."[9]

- Here's another: "I had a parent call me at 6:30 in the evening asking why I hadn't been able to heat up her child's chicken pot pie in the teacher's lounge microwave during lunch. When I informed her that it was my lunch time and also not a service we offered at the school, she responded by asking how her child was supposed to have a hot meal. I suggested she get in line with the other half of the class each day that got a free HOT lunch from the cafeteria."[10]

These last two examples show how some parents think of teachers. In their view, teachers are the parents' employees and should therefore do what parents demand. When teachers resist, entitled parents become irate. In their view, the natural order of things has been upended. What's more, the parents' children watch all this and learn from it. They are receiving early lessons in entitlement.

Examples could easily be multiplied, and some would also include entitled teachers. In any case, what the examples would show is that entitlement blocks gratitude. When I feel entitled, my good things lose their status as gifts. Good things are merely what's owed to a person of my importance. When I am denied something I think I'm entitled to, I resent it.

Living in a Meritocracy

Could it be that the very structure of society breeds both entitlement and resentment and therefore suppresses gratitude?

In *The Tyranny of Merit,* Michael J. Sandel says that in an era of global openness and competition, success depends on having talent, a first-rate education, and a strong work ethic. Supposedly everyone has equal opportunity. The result is that those who are successful believe they have earned their success and therefore deserve it. Given the assumption of equal opportunity, "those who are left behind deserve their fate as well."[11] This is meritocracy, and Sandel wants to persuade us that it is a tyrant.

To take one example, Sandel describes affluent American kids who are depressed, anxious, and hooked on drugs. Their condition seems situational. They're pushed by hovering parents who regard their child's admission to Harvard as a shining page in the parents' own book. Parents hope to have this page ready for cocktail parties, which they want to attend while smug with the knowledge that their kid got into Harvard, not the University of Eastern West Virginia at Seltzer Springs.

This puts their high school kids under enormous pressure to succeed. These kids are often miserable. They plunge themselves into an overloaded schedule of band, track, student council, regular courses, and AP courses, plus any creative venture outside school that might give them an edge. All this drives them mercilessly, robbing them of joy and of sleep. They become perfectionists, obsessed with detail in a way that actually interferes with their performance. And if they do get into a competitive college such as Harvard, they have to compete all over again—even to get into a club.[12]

Throughout, kids striving for success can't elude the feeling that they are not so much their parents' child as their parents' project and that their parents' love is conditional on their success. The parents' pride and the kids' resentment—prime results of meritocracy at work—make gratitude only an occasional visitor in the home.

Cynicism. Self-sufficiency. Greed. Apathy. Resentment. Entitlement. So many ways to stop gratitude! You would almost think that the forces of evil have a special purpose in preventing us from being grateful. Considering all these obstacles to gratitude, it seems a wonder that anybody still has it. And yet many folks plainly do. They thank God, family members, and friends every day. They keep a list of all their blessings and rejoice over them. They may be only moderately well off but feel rich. They develop antidotes for the sins that block gratitude. And they practice the measures for getting gratitude that we explored in chapter 2.

Time now to see some of the good things that come to such folks just because they are thankful people.

What Happens to Me
If I Am Grateful?

John Claypool was a gifted Christian preacher, writer, and speaker who ministered in Southern Baptist and Episcopal churches and fought for the civil rights movement in the mid-1960s. There was power in his words, which were never more eloquent than when he preached four weeks after his young daughter's death from leukemia in 1970.

Consolation

Laura Lue Claypool was ten years old when she died. Her father and mother were devastated. Like any loving parent, John Claypool was overcome by a mix of horror, bitterness, and fear. He was afraid he wouldn't know how to live in a world turned incomprehensible to him. If "this is my Father's world," as the hymn says, then how in this world can a lovely ten-year-old girl be ravaged by cancer till she has to bite on

45

a rag because of the agony? She would beg her dad "to pray to God to take away that awful pain," Claypool said, and "I would kneel down beside her bed and pray with all the faith and conviction of my soul, and nothing would happen except the pain continuing to rage on."[1]

John Claypool preached about the tragedy to his congregation at Crescent Hill Baptist Church in Louisville. It had been only weeks since Laura Lue's death, and he was still broken and numb. Bathed in the love and sorrow of his congregation, he fought to come to terms with what had happened.

He saw, almost at once, that two familiar routes through his grief would come to a dead end. According to the first, when tragedy strikes we should simply resign ourselves to it. It's God's will, people say, and there's nothing we can do but submit to it. Don't question it. Don't rail against it. Just surrender and make the best of it.

In his sermon, Claypool rejects this advice. God isn't simply a brute force. We aren't stoics trying to live unperturbed by such a force. We are children of God, and when we suffer tragedy we lament to God. Didn't Jesus himself agonize with God in Gethsemane? Didn't Jesus cry out to God on the cross, "Why have you forsaken me?" (Matt. 27:46). This is plainly a protest. It's almost an accusation.[2]

If simple submission to tragedy won't do for a Christian, how about a second route through tragedy? What if we say

> "There is more honest faith in an act of questioning than in the act of silent submission, for implicit in the very asking is the faith that some light can be given."
>
> —John Claypool[a]

46

that the way to survive devastation in our lives is to adopt a skeptic's nihilism? Claypool's temptation along this line was to sink to the conclusion that life was pointless, absurd, utterly without purpose and ultimate love. Isn't this what the tortured death of a lovely ten-year-old suggests?

But Claypool couldn't follow this route to the end either. Through his suffering, he experienced so much goodness that he simply couldn't conclude that life was absurd. People in the hospital, in church, in the community came to his side with overwhelming love and kindness. All had looked so dark. But right in the middle was all this light.

In the end John Claypool looked for—and found—a third route through his grief. He came to see that Laura Lue had been God's gift to him and that, alongside his grief, he needed gratitude for this marvelous gift. The gift had lasted only ten years, but what years they had been! After his daughter's death, Claypool savored memories of Laura Lue— things she had said, things they had done together, things she had cherished.[3] He testified to his congregation that if they wanted to help him with his loss, they might help him recall who Laura Lue was and how she had been a gift to them all.

The story of Laura Lue reminds me that if I have gratitude, it may console me in my loss of a loved one. If I lose someone I love, what I will pray, and what I hope others will pray for me, is that over time my gratitude will start to overshadow my grief. If it does, I will begin to mend. The loss hurts, but gratitude heals. Isn't this remarkable? God has arranged the world such that gratitude for good things and persons is not only right and fitting. It's also a powerful consolation when we lose them.

Contentment

As we've already seen, my gratitude makes me content. Gratitude turns what I have into enough. This works because grateful and contented people are blessed with a realistic outlook. Their expectations are duly limited. In J. R. R. Tolkien's *The Lord of the Rings,* the wise and righteous Gandalf observes at one point that good people may conquer some evils, but not all of them and only for the time being:

> It is not our part to master all the tides of the world, but to do what is in us for the succor of those years wherein we are set, uprooting the evil in the fields that we know, so that those who live after may have clean earth to till. What weather they shall have is not ours to rule.[4]

So it is with us. As we mature we learn not to expect too much. We expect our education, for example, to give us knowledge. That's what the tuition pays for. But, if we are realistic, we don't expect our education—all by itself—to give us wisdom. To acquire wisdom, we're going to have to live awhile. If we are married, we expect our marriage to give us pleasure, but we don't expect that it will give us ecstasy. If we have a good job, we expect it to give us a living, maybe satisfaction, but we don't expect it will give us total fulfillment. For total fulfillment we would need the kingdom of God to come. In all three cases, a realistic outlook saves us from a lot of disappointment.

Realistic expectations are an exhibit of humility. Humble people are down to earth.[5] They have their feet on the ground. They don't expect their children to be rock stars. They don't expect their friends to bow to them. They don't expect God to answer all their questions. Of course they have hopes, but their hopes have limits. Their realistic outlook lets them be

Twenty-first-century Christians in China are deeply grateful for remarkable growth in conversions and resources. These things reassure them that the Holy Spirit is at work among them. But these same Christians do not expect their government to quit its repressive practices anytime soon.[b]

grateful for small gifts and ordinary occasions. Their gratitude gives them contentment because it turns what they have into enough.

Joy

In the first chapter I said that gratitude is a glad sense of being gifted with something by someone and of thus being indebted to the giver. I think we may now call this gladness "joy" when the gift is more than trivial. Let's say joy is strong gladness. I might not respond with joy if you praise my shoes, but I might if you praise my kindness. That's a compliment with real weight, and my gladness at receiving it could easily rise to the level of joy.

I suppose we most often think of joyful gratitude in connection with family and friends. A good marriage can deliver joy to both spouses through immense gratitude for the other's compassion, thoughtfulness, reliability, and much else. Children and parents and friends can bring us joy for the same reasons.

For Christians, grateful joy centers on Jesus Christ, God's Son, our Lord. He is the supreme gift. The most famous verse in the Bible says so, in a verse that millions have memorized: "God so loved the world that he gave his only Son, so that everyone who believes in him may not perish but may have eternal life" (John 3:16). At Jesus's birth an angel made history's premier announcement to a group of shepherds: "I am bringing you good news of great joy for all the people" (Luke 2:10).

At Christmas celebrations, Christians *sing* their joy. It's not enough to *say* it. Our hearts are full and we need to sing our hearts out. We need to *raise* our voices. "Joy to the world, the Lord is come! Let earth receive her King. . . . Joy to the earth, the Savior reigns! Let all their songs employ, while fields and floods, rocks, hills, and plains, repeat the sounding joy."[6]

At Easter we repeat the sounding joy: "Alleluia, alleluia! Hearts to heaven and voices raise. Sing to God a hymn of gladness, sing to God a hymn of praise."[7] Again, "Come, you faithful, raise the strain of triumphant gladness!"[8] And, famously, again:

> Christ the Lord is risen today, Alleluia!
> All creation join to say, Alleluia!
> Raise your joys and triumphs high, Alleluia!
> Sing, O heavens, and earth reply, Alleluia![9]

Thanksgiving for our Savior and joyful expression of it in song constitute stellar Christian worship. For Christians, this is their groove, their sweet spot, a sublime way for them to act in character. Gratitude generates joy, and joy wants to sing.

Generosity

When in 2001 my denomination asked me to become president of Calvin Theological Seminary, I hesitated. This was plainly an administrative post and I thought my gifts lay elsewhere. Moreover, one of the biggest parts of the job would be to raise money, a prospect that intimidated me a little.

But, after praying about the matter and discussing it with my wife Kathleen and close friends, I accepted my church's call and went off to New Presidents' School[10] to learn how to be a president. We had highly informative lessons in fundraising. During one of them, a veteran president told of a couple who had asked him a heavy question. If they were to give $3 million for his seminary's chapel, would he change its name? Yes! he told them. Yes, indeed! In fact, for $3 million he'd change *his* name. Then he added something I've never forgotten. He said that conscientious donors are always looking for good reasons to give. They *want* to give, and if they love your seminary's mission and trust you as its leader, they'll do it.

I found this counsel confirmed on the job. So many times after I had laid out my seminary's need for donors and asked them for help, people would say something to this effect: "God has blessed us beyond our deserving, beyond our hopes. So, yes, of course we'll help." Sometimes donors would say their money wasn't really theirs. It was God's money given to them with trust that they'd give it away well.

In any case, the link between donors' gratitude and their generosity was perfectly clear. And you can find it at the top levels of philanthropy. In 2010 Warren Buffett, one of the greatest philanthropists in the world, asked Bill Gates of Microsoft fame to join him in making "The Giving Pledge," a promise to give away the bulk of their wealth in their lifetime. Gates agreed, and over two hundred other billionaires in the world have since signed on. In establishing the pledge, Buffett wrote this:

> The reaction of my family and me to our extraordinary good fortune is not guilt, but rather gratitude. . . . Keep all we can conceivably need and distribute the rest to society, for its needs. My pledge starts us down that course.[11]

I suppose few will be surprised that gratitude tends to produce generosity. You might be a little more surprised to learn that the link between them is hardwired into our brains. Christina Karns, a research psychologist at the University of Oregon, studies social neuroscience. To test for a link between gratitude and generosity, she composed a study in which subjects were given a sum of money and told that a computer would randomly assign this money either to themselves or to a charity.[12] Half the subjects were assigned to keep a gratitude journal for three weeks about the various good things in their lives.

After three weeks, Karns scanned the brains of all the subjects whose money had been assigned to charity. The brains of those who had kept a journal showed significantly increased activity in the reward centers of the brain—the regions that give us a dose of feel-good neurotransmitters. It turns out that if we are grateful, our brains will love us if we are also generous. Our Creator's ingenuity has wired our brains this way.

Christina Karns's work is a fine example of what's called "positive psychology," a movement begun by Martin Seligman in 1998. Psychology had traditionally focused on diseased states of mind and emotion—on neuroses such as obsessive-compulsive disorder and psychoses such as schizophrenia. Frustrated by the exclusively negative cast of psychological studies, Seligman proposed that psychologists should also study positive states and traits, such as happiness, compassion, and gratitude.[13]

Positive psychologists have by now published thousands of pages of such studies, making enormous contributions to the psychological health of ordinary people. One of the main proposals of positive psychology is that a basic shift in our perspective, our outlook on life, can do remarkable things for our sense of well-being.[14]

In particular, positive psychologists have discovered some of the wonderful benefits of gratitude. Experience may teach us that gratitude can produce (or at least predict) contentment, joy, and generosity. But positive psychologists have documented these benefits in their psychological research.

Psychologist Charlotte vanOyen-Witvliet and her colleagues have shown that gratitude predicts hope and general happiness—two states unmistakably characteristic of well-being—and that gratitude correlates with accountability. Grateful people are hopeful and happy, but they are also fair: they take responsibility for giving others their due.[15]

Healthier Hearts

Positive psychologists can also document purely physical benefits of gratitude, not just states of mind. In a piece for NPR, journalist Patti Neighmond used the run-up to Thanksgiving Day 2015 to reflect on the heart benefits of gratitude.[16] She cited the work of Paul Mills, who teaches family medicine and public health at the University of California, San Diego, School of Medicine. Mills studies heart health, heart disease, and the behaviors that affect them. He wondered whether it wasn't just behaviors but also attitudes and outlooks that might affect our hearts for good or ill. In particular, he wondered about gratitude.

So Mills composed and conducted a test. He gathered a group of 186 senior citizens with a history of heart issues—high blood pressure, heart infection, or heart attack—and had them rate their gratitude on a standard questionnaire. He then tested the blood of the participants, looking for plaque in their arteries.

The results were encouraging. Mills determined that the most grateful participants had the lowest levels of plaque, a clear sign of healthier hearts.

As Neighmond tells it, Mills followed up with a study of forty heart patients with inflammation and heart arrhythmia. He assigned daily journaling to half of them, asking them to note the things they were grateful for. People made a wide variety of entries, from interactions with their pets to good meals to the tangible benefits brought to their lives by their loved ones.

> After two months, Mills retested all 40 patients and found health benefits for the patients who wrote in their journals. Inflammation levels were reduced, and heart rhythm improved. And when he compared their heart disease risk before and after journal writing, there was a decrease in risk after two months of writing in their journals.[17]

How does gratitude contribute to healthy hearts? One good possibility, Mills thinks, is that gratitude lowers stress—a major contributor to heart disease. "Taking the time to focus on what you are thankful for, letting that sense of gratitude wash over you—this helps us manage and cope," Mills says.[18]

Lower Blood Pressure

While we're in the heart department, we should also note another key benefit of gratitude. Researchers have documented that gratitude predicts lower blood pressure. This is remarkable—and important. We can all gauge the importance of our blood pressure by the mere fact that at every visit to the doctor's office we can expect our blood pressure to be taken. If the pressure is too high, we may be given a prescription to lower it. This is no surprise. Blood pressure is a major factor in blood health—which is a major factor in general health.

Let's remind ourselves why. Our blood is rich with oxygen and such nutrients as the minerals, vitamins, and glucose needed by our organs and tissues. To get where it needs to go, our blood must be under pressure. If our arteries are stiff or blocked, our blood pressure rises, and if it rises too high, we are at risk of heart attack or stroke. The good news is that various diet and lifestyle changes can lower blood pressure, as can conventionally prescribed medications.

But being grateful does the trick too. In 2021 three researchers conducted a study to test the effect of gratitude on blood pressure.[19] They equipped participants with a special app on their phone that included an optic sensor to record their heart rate and blood pressure. At each of numerous check-ins over a length of time, participants would respond to a series of questions about their health behaviors, stress levels, daily experiences, and gratitude. Gratitude was measured with a standard six-item gratitude questionnaire that required participants to respond to statements such as "I have so much in life to be thankful for" and "I am grateful to a wide variety of people."

Responses were recorded on a seven-point scale (1 = strongly disagree, 7 = strongly agree).

The results of the test were impressive. Grateful people turned out to have notably lower blood pressure—and this was true not just in a single check-in measurement but also in repeated measurements over a significant length of time. According to the test, gratitude causes, or at least predicts, lower blood pressure.

A Splendid Array of Other Benefits

In 2018 the Greater Good Science Center at University of California, Berkeley, prepared a report for the John Templeton Foundation titled "The Science of Gratitude."[20] Citing a host of scientific studies, the report summarizes what's known to date about the benefits of gratitude. In addition to lower blood pressure and healthier hearts, grateful people enjoy an eye-opening number of other benefits.

- They experience less depression and anxiety.
- They sleep longer and better and awaken more refreshed.
- They have lower levels of systemic inflammation.
- They have higher levels of happiness and satisfaction with their lives.
- They are less prone to materialism.
- They are less prone to workplace burnout.
- They are more resilient after traumatic events.
- They are more patient.

- They are more "prosocial"—more benevolent, more supportive of others.
- They form and maintain strong relationships more consistently.

This is a potent array of benefits. Any of us thinking of gratitude as little more than a social nicety should find this list to be a wake-up call.

In an important article in *Scientific American*, Scott Barry Kaufman reports his attempt to answer the question, "Which character strengths are most predictive of well-being?"[21] In positive psychology, a standard description of well-being is one proposed by Martin Seligman. It's called the PERMA model, and it includes five elements:

- **P**ositive emotion, such as joy, hope, and love.
- **E**ngagement, or the ability to lose yourself in healthy activities.
- **R**elationships in which you get respect, support, and love.
- **M**eaning or purpose in life.
- **A**ccomplishment, or competence in achieving goals.

In his study, Kaufman and his associates collected data on 517 people and analyzed it. What they found first was that the five elements of PERMA come as a package. Anybody who has any of them is likely to have all of them.

In further analysis, Kaufman found that hope, love, and love of learning were exceptional predictors of well-being, but that *"the single best predictor of well-being was gratitude."*[22]

Taken together, the UC Berkeley and Kaufman reports show why gratitude is such an important virtue. Besides being prominent in Scripture as the fitting response to God's mighty acts, besides being prominent in worship in prayer and sacrament, gratitude appears to be the single virtue most prominently associated with human flourishing.

I'll note once again that we can spot our Creator's ingenuity in arranging life this way—so that doing what's right turns out also to be doing what's healthy and wise. It's right to be grateful for the gifts that come to us. Or, as the *Book of Common Prayer* has it with respect to thanking God, it is "very meet, right, and our bounden duty."[23] But in God's world, if we do our duty we also thrive. And that's a remarkable fact.

No wonder Scripture so urgently calls us to thankfulness.

A Self-Help Project?

Publicity about the power of gratitude to improve ourselves has caused some commentators to take a step back. In an opinion piece in the *New York Times*, Barbara Ehrenreich looks at all the people recommending gratitude for its health benefits and says, in effect, Wait a minute! Isn't gratitude supposed to be the fitting response to generosity? Aren't there actual people out there who harvest our food, get it to market, and present it to us for our dinner table? Shouldn't the focus be on them? So what's all this fuss about how being grateful helps *us*?[24]

Look, says Ehrenreich, gratitude enthusiasts tell us to take a scenic walk, post a sticky note of gratitude on our mirror, count our blessings, or rig our computer to display a gratitude reminder every morning. "Who is interacting here? 'You' and 'you.'" Think about it!

It's possible to achieve the recommended levels of gratitude without spending a penny or uttering a word. All you have to do is to generate, within yourself, the good feelings associated with gratitude, and then bask in its warm, comforting glow. If there is any loving involved in this, it is self-love.[25]

Ehrenreich has a point, and it's a sharp one. Turning gratitude into a self-help hustle is a corruption. We should not be surprised that sinfulness can corrupt even virtues. In fact, the forces of evil can achieve their worst by corrupting our faith and virtues. They achieve their worst by corrupting our best.

Gratitude is no exception. Think of Jesus's story of the Pharisee and the tax collector who went up to the temple to pray. The Pharisee was "standing by himself" as he prayed, "God, I thank you that I am not like other people: thieves, rogues, adulterers, or even like this tax collector" (Luke 18:11). "I thank you that I am not like other people." Here self-righteousness masquerades as gratitude.

That's one form of corrupt gratitude. Another is turning faithful thanks for gifts into a self-improvement project. If I am biblically disciplined, I won't do this. I'll offer my thanks to God and to generous brothers and sisters because it is right.

But it is not wrong for me to notice that if I do this, I'll also sleep better.

5

Biblical Themes

In 1988 veteran CBS journalist Charles Kuralt was in Moscow to cover the summit meeting of President Ronald Reagan and Mikhail Gorbachev, chairman of the Soviet Union.[1] While Kuralt was there, he met a retired Russian dentist who had a story to tell.

Dr. Nikita Aseyev had waited for over forty years to tell his story. During the Second World War, Dr. Aseyev had been captured by the Germans and imprisoned in Stalag 3-B, a concentration camp in Furstenberg on the Oder River. The Germans treated him and his Russian compatriots miserably. They provided starvation rations of only one liter of turnip soup per day. The inevitable result: Russians began to die, first by the tens and then by the hundreds.

Across a wire fence from the Russians, eight thousand American prisoners were faring better because their captors allowed the Red Cross to deliver food parcels to them once a week. Dr. Aseyev found out about this during his supervised visits to the American side to fix teeth. On one visit, two brothers, Michael and Peter Wowczuk, proposed that they and the other Americans share their Red Cross provisions with the Russians.

Once a week, late at night, the Americans would throw food parcels over the fence to the Russians—enough parcels to keep the Russians from starving. The Americans knew they were risking their lives to do this. If discovered, they would have been shot.

When the Germans finally figured out what was going on, they assembled the American prisoners on their parade ground and demanded from each one of them the name of the Russian who had organized the relief plot. As Charles Kuralt tells the story, here's what happened:

> For three hours in the sun, with nothing to drink, the Americans stood in absolute silence. They stood there with clenched lips. The German officers threatened them with severe reprisal. They stood in silence. Not a word was spoken. Not one American gave the name of the Russian, Dr. Aseyev.[2]

Dr. Aseyev survived the war, wrote down the names of eleven American heroes who had saved his life and the lives of his compatriots, and delivered them to Charles Kuralt on the day they met. He told Kuralt that he had been waiting for over forty years with those names—waiting to publicize them to an American news source, waiting to thank the brave and compassionate Americans who had risked everything for him.

After Kuralt's story about all this had aired on television, one of the American heroes, William Jarema of New York, flew to Moscow to meet with Dr. Aseyev. As they embraced and wept, neither could speak. "No words could find their way to the surface through all the emotions."[3]

Memory and Gratitude

Kuralt's story reminds me of the power of memory in triggering gratitude. Dr. Aseyev had never forgotten how those compassionate Americans had saved his life. Few of us have memories as dramatic as those of Dr. Aseyev. Still, we know the connection between memory and gratitude. When we remember good things others have done for us, we feel gratitude all over again for those people.

Gratitude triggered by the memory of goodness is a classic biblical pattern. As we've seen, this is the structure of Passover seders with their Dayenu memories of God's great acts of deliverance. Following suit, we Christians preserve this pattern in the Eucharist or Lord's Supper with its Great Prayer of Thanksgiving.

Where gratitude is concerned, the first biblical theme to consider is that God calls Israel and the church to remember how much they have to give thanks for. Accordingly, God calls believers back to these memories when they forget and lapse into ingratitude and complaint.

We can see the pattern with Israel in the wilderness. God has rescued Israel from bondage in Egypt, but she has not yet reached the promised land. At Mount Sinai God delivers the Ten Commandments to Moses, who then passes them

"If He had given us their wealth and had not split the sea for us—Dayenu, it would have been enough!

"If He had split the sea for us and had not taken us through it on dry land—Dayenu, it would have been enough!"[a]

on to the Israelites. As recorded in Deuteronomy, the first commandment presents God as liberator: "I am the LORD your God, who brought you out of the land of Egypt, out of the house of slavery; you shall have no other gods before me" (Deut. 5:6–7). A few commandments later, God tells the Israelites to "observe the sabbath day and keep it holy" (v. 12) and goes on to prohibit work on the sabbath by everybody in the household, including an Israelite's servants. They are to get the day off. Even Israel's livestock are to get the day off. The reason for the prohibition is instructive:

> Remember that you were a slave in the land of Egypt, and the LORD your God brought you out from there with a mighty hand and an outstretched arm; therefore the LORD your God commanded you to keep the sabbath day. (v. 15)

It would be hard to exaggerate the importance of the exodus deliverance in the rest of the Bible. God's biblical reputation becomes that of the exodus God. God's people are the exodus people. The psalms that praise or thank God for deliverance often appear to have the exodus in mind.[4] Psalm 9, for example, tells of God's "wonderful deeds" and praises God for them. To Israel, the exodus would have headed the list of such deeds. Such a reading would have been confirmed as the psalmist goes on to tell how his enemies "turned back," how they "stumbled and perished before you" (vv. 1–3). This description recalls what happened in the exodus when the Egyptians pursued Israel into the Red Sea.

Israel is called to remember God's "mighty hand and outstretched arm" in delivering them from the Egyptians and to thank God for their freedom. Sad to say, Israel's record of gratitude after the exodus is spotty. During the Israelites' trip through the wilderness to Mount Sinai, more and more of them line up at the complaint window to kvetch about food and water shortages. At one point the Israelites romanticize their slavery in Egypt by claiming they had enjoyed plenty of leisure there to sit around pots of meat and eat their fill. Maybe they should have died there! Then at least they could have died on a full stomach (Exod. 16:3)!

When Moses and the people arrive at Mount Sinai, Moses climbs the mountain to commune with God while the people wait below for him to come down. Then they wait some more. Finally, Israel's impatience and ingratitude get the best of them. They tell Moses's brother Aaron that they've had it. Their tone is contemptuous and dismissive. Look, they say, as for "this Moses" who brought us here, we haven't any idea what's happened to him. But we can't just sit out here in the middle of nowhere. If Moses's God is a fairy tale, then we need a new god.

Aaron thinks back to the religion market in Egypt and recalls that the Egyptians were fairly satisfied with their cattle gods. So Aaron fashions a golden calf for the Israelites and, in the ultimate blasphemy, tells them that *this* is the god "who brought you up out of the land of Egypt!" (Exod. 32:4). Mere months after God rescued Israel from Egypt, the people have already forgotten. Worse, they have absurdly swapped their liberator for a little gold, cud-chewing stud.[5]

We can imagine Moses's sense of futility after he comes down the mountain with the tablets of the Ten Commandments. The first commandment says, "You shall have no other gods before me," but now Moses hears his people shouting and sees them dancing around the golden calf.[6] Having witnessed this, an exasperated Moses is now doubly vigilant about the

65

need for Israel to remember God's goodness and give thanks for it.

As they prepare to enter the promised land, he warns the people one last time:

> Take care that you do not forget the LORD your God. . . . When you have eaten your fill and have built fine houses and live in them, and when your herds and flocks have multiplied . . . then do not exalt yourself, forgetting the LORD your God, who brought you out of the land of Egypt, out of the house of slavery. . . . Do not say to yourself, 'My power and the might of my own hand have gotten me this wealth.' But remember the LORD your God, for it is he who gives you power to get wealth, so that he may confirm his covenant that he swore to your ancestors. (Deut. 8:11–18)[7]

All throughout Scripture, this theme beats like a drum. God has done great things for you. Remember! Do not forget! I write this to remind you! By way of reminder, all throughout Scripture its writers urge God's people to praise God, to thank God, to glorify God.

And, of course, we Christians today have taken notice. That's why our Scripture readings in worship services often include a reminder of the mighty acts of God. That's why our prayers include acclamation, praise, thanksgiving. That's why Christian sermons often include these same themes.

Thankfulness Is Part of "Rising with Christ"

Giving thanks is a regular upbeat in the rhythm of a healthy Christian life. The psalms ring with thanksgiving for the whole catalog of God's goods and services. For God's rescue work, for the law that puts spine in our lives, for the tender mercies of God that settle in around us even when we have shamed ourselves—for these things, and so much more, the poets of God send up their thanks like thousands of helium balloons.

The psalms are mostly prayers and calls to prayer. But Paul does something else. Paul proclaims the great dying and rising events of Christ, binds us to these events, and describes the style of life that naturally follows.

Every Christian knows that our faith centers on Jesus's death and resurrection. These are the mightiest of God's mighty acts and the most important exhibits of God's goodness. What many Christians don't know is that Jesus did not die and rise alone. All of us believers died and rose with him.[8] This is one of the greatest of St. Paul's teachings—and, at first, one of the strangest.

To understand it, we need to see that Paul has several things in mind when he speaks of us dying and rising with Christ.[9]

1. We died and rose when he did. He *represented* us when he died and rose. He took our sins upon him, such that when he died, so did—in God's eyes—our old and sinful self. When he rose, so did—in God's eyes—our new and blameless self. This teaching answers the question posed so soulfully by the African American spiritual "Were You There When They Crucified My Lord?" It's a rhetorical question with an implied yes that prompts the anguished response, "Oh, sometimes it causes me to tremble, tremble, tremble."

2. We died and rose with Christ in our baptism, which signals and pledges that Jesus's death and resurrection really are for us. How does baptism do this? The best way is by immersion, in which we reenact the dying and rising of Jesus. When the minister plunges us underwater, we go down into

death like Christ. When the minister lifts us up and out of the water, we rise to life like Christ.[10] By immersion or by the less vivid method of sprinkling, baptism unites us with Christ, identifies us with Christ, binds us to Christ, and says that his events are *our* events too.

3. Since we have already died and risen with Christ, says Paul, we ought to keep the rhythm going. We ought to *keep on* dying and rising with Christ by putting to death our old self, with all its malice and resentment, and rising to life in our new self with all its compassion, kindness, and *thankfulness*. "So if you have been raised with Christ," says Paul, "be thankful." Sing your hearts out "with gratitude." In fact, "do everything in the name of the Lord Jesus, giving thanks to God the Father through him" (Col. 3:1, 15–17).

Three times in a row Paul urges thanksgiving as a natural feature of our resurrected character.

Why? What's the point? Surely not simply to keep the goods flowing, as if we were caged rats who had discovered the food lever. What's the point of thankfulness? Surely not to fulfill some unstated contract with God: We like goods. God likes thanks. Even Steven.

No, thankfulness in the rhythm of Christian life falls instead into a category that is easier to illustrate than to define. Thankfulness falls into the category of what is *fitting* for grateful people. Fittingness. In so many ways God is a giver. How fitting it is that we should, so to speak, return the compliment. God gives and we give back. Among the few things we *have* to give back is the kind of hearty thanks that is right and proper and fitting.

In sum, we died and rose with Christ when he did. We die and rise with Christ in our baptism. And we do it every day when we put our ingratitude to death and let our gratitude come to life.

I'll add something I find remarkable. When Paul says we have been raised with Christ, he says we should "clothe ourselves" with the virtues of Christ—with compassion, kindness, humility, gentleness, patience, forbearance, forgivingness, love, and peace. Then, as we just saw, Paul tells us three times in a row to be thankful (Col. 3:1, 12–17). Why does he say we should "clothe ourselves" with gratitude?

He almost surely has in mind how early Christians coming up from the water of baptism were handed a new, clean garment to symbolize their new, clean life. It's their baptismal robe. Paul's point is that gratitude *fits* people who have been raised with Christ. Gratitude is part of the *family uniform* of the people of God.

Thankfulness Is Part of the Image of God

That we have died and risen with Christ means we are "in Christ," in union with Christ. This is central to our identity as human beings—so central that if we are hungry or thirsty or sick and a compassionate brother or sister ministers to us, Jesus Christ sees them as having ministered to *him* (Matt. 25:31–40).

If being in union with Christ is central to our identity, so is the fact that we have been created in the image of God. Most of us are aware of this remarkable fact, but some of us may be a little fuzzy on what it means.

It means at least three things, the last one bearing directly on how we should think of gratitude.

1. At the climax of the story of creation in Genesis 1, God says, "Let us make humankind in our image, according to our

likeness; and let them have dominion" over the rest of creation (1:26). The idea is that God, the king of creation, deputizes us to play a role in exercising responsible dominion within the world. This is no license for human beings to lord it over creation by abusing animals and fouling streams. Just the opposite. Humans represent God by loving creation, by practicing intelligent animal husbandry and land management, by letting creation unfold under their faithful stewardship. When they do this, they are like God!

2. We are also like God when we live in loving fellowship with each other. God is a triune society of three loving, communing persons, and we are like God when we commune with each other in love and loyalty. The image of God is thus social, not just individual, and its chief example—however imperfect—is the church. This explains why Jesus in John 17 and Paul, throughout his letters, are so keenly concerned with the unity of the church. Only in unity can the church be like the triune God.

3. We are like God when we clothe ourselves with the virtues of Christ—compassion, kindness, humility, gentleness, patience, forbearance, forgiveness, love, peace, and gratitude (Col. 3:12–17). Jesus Christ is himself the preeminent image of God the Father. He is the exegesis of God who bears the very stamp of the divine nature and who exists "in the form of God" (Phil. 2:6; see also Col. 1:15; John 1:18; Heb. 1:3). Because Jesus has this supreme status, we believers must conform ourselves to him (Rom. 8:29; 2 Cor. 3:18).

How would we do that?

- By weeping with a friend who has been humiliated by losing a much-needed job.

- By commending a timid colleague for work about which they feel incompetent.
- By meeting others as a fellow traveler, not a prima donna.
- By meeting a hard word with a soft one.
- By absorbing irritants without becoming irritated.
- By putting up with people who drive us nuts.
- By dropping anger against someone even when we have a right to it.
- By pursuing social justice for people we don't even know.
- By serving as mediator between two friends who need to be reconciled.
- By thanking God for everything good in our lives.

There they are, examples of the virtues of Christ: compassion, kindness, humility, gentleness, patience, forbearance, forgiveness, love, peace, and gratitude. By clothing ourselves with these virtues, we are like Jesus and therefore like God.

It's striking that in passages where Scripture lays out the virtues of Christ and calls us to cultivate them, it regards our doing so as a *renewal* of the image of God. Ephesians 4 is classic in this respect. Like Colossians 3, it uses the imagery of clothing to summon us to Christlikeness:

> You were taught to put away your former way of life, your old self . . . and to be renewed in the spirit of your minds, and to clothe yourselves with the new self, created according to the likeness of God in true righteousness and holiness. (Eph. 4:22–24)

Here the image of God consists in "true righteousness and holiness." And that makes perfect sense: God is famous for these qualities, and human beings are notorious for having lost them in the fall. Our first parents were created morally good. Their lapse into unbelief, pride, and disobedience cost them their righteousness.

But now we are to clothe ourselves "with the new self," the Christlike self, the virtues-of-Christ self that is a *second* creation by God. This second creation recovers our original righteousness and thus renews the image of God in us. What are the virtues of this new self with which we are to clothe ourselves? The same ones Paul lists in Colossians 3, including gratitude; plus the ones from Ephesians 4–5, including truthfulness, kindness, and gratitude; plus the ones from Galatians 5, the fruit of the Spirit; plus the ones from Romans 12, including perseverance and hospitality.[11] All these lists are partly overlapping samples of the virtues of Christ that, even partially acquired, constitute the renewed image of God in believers.

Gratitude Is a Ligament of Church Unity

A favorite Pauline image of the church is the body of Christ, with Christ as the head of the body (1 Cor. 12:12–27; Rom. 12:4–5; Col. 1:18, 24). Displaying his ever-present concern for the unity of the church, Paul even speaks of it as the body of Christ held together by means of its "ligaments and sinews" (Col. 2:19). Paul says this just before he lists, in the very next chapter, the virtues of Christ that reinforce our union with Christ.

I think we understand. As we saw earlier, a Christian's baptism unites them with Christ in his death and resurrection. Baptism is a church sacrament that says the person baptized is one of us—a person in union with Christ. Union with Christ is ipso facto union with others, and a more perfect union with others will require a lot of virtue on the part of the members.

Thus Paul counsels humility because Christians need to respect each other's dignity and each other's complementary gifts to function as a healthy body. Paul exhorts forgivingness because we can't have a reconciling community unless those who have been forgiven by God forgive each other. Paul also counsels believers to "weep with those who weep," not particularly because compassion is a sign that a person possesses a full range of emotions (and that a man who can cry is an up-to-date type of guy) but because compassion is the kind of empathy that binds believers together.

Gratitude, too, promotes unity in the church. Nothing in the church defeats rivalry and cliques better than gratitude— mutual gratitude to Christ and mutual gratitude for each other. What do you suppose was the effect in Paul's churches of the fact that he greeted them in his letters with an outpouring of love and gratitude?

- "I give thanks to my God always for you." (1 Cor. 1:4)
- "I do not cease to give thanks for you as I remember you in my prayers." (Eph. 1:16)
- "I thank my God every time I remember you, constantly praying with joy in every one of my prayers for all of you, because of your sharing in the gospel from the first day until now. . . . God is my witness, how I long for all of you with the compassion of Christ Jesus." (Phil. 1:3–5, 8)

I remember you. I pray for you. I long for you. I thank God for you. Gratitude in the church is a sturdy ligament of the body of Christ. It binds everybody together.

We're now in a position to see something wonderful. If I am grateful to God and to others, I give evidence of a healthy inner life. If I have a healthy inner life, I am strong enough to tell others how grateful I am for them. If they are fellow members of the church, and if they do the same for still others, the church becomes unified and strong. If the church becomes unified and strong, it becomes a more powerful instrument of the kingdom of God. And if the kingdom of God comes in its fullness, created life in concert with God reaches its climax.

The first link in this golden chain is simple gratitude.

6

Thank God! Why?

There's a familiar old story that often comes to my mind when I'm thinking of God's goodness in ordinary life.[1] According to the story, an American CEO on vacation in Mexico was visiting a village on the Gulf Coast. As he watched, a small boat returned from a fishing run and tied up at the dock.

A single fisherman stepped up on the dock with his catch—three good-sized yellowfin tuna. The American, impressed with the quality of the catch, asked the Mexican how long it had taken him to snag them.

"Not long at all," said the fisherman.

"So, why didn't you stay out there a while longer?" asked the CEO.

"These are enough to feed me and my family for now," said the Mexican.

"OK," said the American, "but what do you do the rest of the time then?"

"Oh," said the Mexican, "I enjoy my good life. I get up when I want to, fish a while, play with my kids, and lie down for a siesta with my wife Maria. At night I walk into the village and see my amigos. We enjoy a little wine and play guitar. Then I go home. I have a full life and I love it."

The businessman was unimpressed. "You're thinking small," he said. "You need a business plan. Start fishing all day, sell a bigger catch, and buy a bigger boat. Then, as your income grows, buy more boats. Build a fleet. Cut out the middleman and sell your catch directly to the processor. As you prosper, become the processor yourself. Open your own cannery. Then you'd own the whole business—from product to distribution. As you grow, you could move your business to Mexico City and then to Los Angeles and eventually to New York."

The Mexican listened and had a question: "How long would all this take?"

The CEO said, "Oh, about 15–20 years."

"But what then?" the fisherman asked.

The American chuckled and said, "Here comes the good part. With the right timing you announce an IPO and get rich off the sale of your company stock and then retire."

"OK, I retire with millions. What then?"

The American said, "Then the best part. You move to a small village on the Gulf of Mexico. You sleep late, fish a little, play with your kids, take siestas with your wife, stroll to the village in the evenings where you would sip wine and play guitar with your amigos."

God's Rescue Work

I think it's natural for our minds to run to special events when we think of God's goodness. Maybe I was trapped by drug addiction but God helped set me free. Or I lost my job in middle age and lost my self-confidence along with it, but God set me on a new and more secure career path. Or my child married someone I didn't think was right for her, and I was terribly worried about it, but by the grace of God their marriage has been just fine.

When I think of these big cases of God's love coming to the rescue, my mind runs to Psalm 103 ("Bless the LORD, O my soul"). Here, you may recall, the psalmist cites some of God's big, liberating work. God forgives my iniquity, heals my diseases, redeems my life from "the Pit," which means God redeems my life from sure destruction. These things all come under the rubric of God's "benefits."

> Bless the LORD, O my soul,
>   and all that is within me,
>   bless his holy name.
> Bless the LORD, O my soul,
>   and do not forget all his benefits. (vv. 1–2)

God's benefit plan includes major rescue work. But not in every instance. God doesn't always come through for us as we had hoped. Our disappointment with God, as Philip Yancey memorably titled it,[2] can be bitter. And I will have much more to say about this at the start of the next chapter.

But even when God *does* come through for us, gifts at this grand level arrive maybe once or twice in a lifetime. What about the rest of the time? What about the Mexican fisherman's satisfaction with his kids and siestas and guitar-playing amigos?

The psalmist seems to have thought of these things too. Yes, God forgives my sins, heals my diseases, and redeems my life from destruction. Famously, the psalmist celebrates such deliverance up front in Psalm 103. What's less often noticed is what he adds next: God "crowns you with steadfast love and mercy" and "satisfies you with good as long as you live."

Everyday Gifts in Ordinary Life

If I ponder this—that God satisfies me with good as long as I live—I can see that we're now in the realm of usual goods, reliable goods, everyday goods in ordinary life. The wonderful truth is that if I am grateful for the small gifts of life day to day, I will never run out of things to be grateful for. My gratitude journal won't have enough slots to record them all.

A little reflection yields a host of these for which I owe God thanks. To aid our reflection, let's go back to David Allan's list from chapter 2:

> Which of these do you have going for you right now? Family. Friends. Love. Health. Freedom from war and natural disaster. Imagination. Community. A roof over our heads. Common decency. Hope. Opportunity. Memories. Financial stability. Favorite places. Days off work. Good weather. The golden age of television. Books. Music. Ice cream. Weekends. A friendly exchange. Something good that happened today. Something bad that didn't happen today. A good cup of coffee.[3]

Not all of us have all these things. But most of us have many of them. Some of them may be much bigger than we know—such as "something bad that didn't happen today."

In any case, you can add your own small gifts to the list. A pillow. Clean sheets. A washing machine. Good detergent. A pair of lightweight wool socks. Comfortable shoes. Three utensils at your plate—a knife, a fork, and a spoon—each with its own distinct function.

The TV show 1883[4] follows the Dutton family—James and Margaret and their daughter Elsa—along with guides and other families as they make the pioneer trek from Texas to Oregon in the year suggested by the title. They travel with horses and covered wagons, and they herd their cattle along the way. From the outset in Fort Worth, the group members have to check each other for smallpox. Once they set out, hardships multiply. Little rain falls on the American prairie, and its vast expanses are broken by few streams and rivers. The Duttons are constantly short of potable water—which they need in abundance not only for themselves but also for their animals. When they do come upon a river, they have to search for a safe place to ford it. Before drinking the water, they have to boil it to kill cholera bacteria.

Meanwhile, as they travel the plains, they must fend off bandits and poisonous snakes. Violent storms leave them defenseless. Lightning can spook their horses, causing them to run away with the wagons and wreck them. At this plodding pace, the wagon train makes such slow progress that food carried from Texas is dwindling. Meanwhile, winter looms ahead.

As they travel, the Duttons regularly pass whitened skeletons and makeshift graves. They can't miss the message: the Oregon Trail is a long, linear graveyard.

As I watch the episodes, I think of all the blessings of ordinary life we have that the Duttons did not: Smallpox vaccine. Plenty of clean drinking water. Safe bridges over rivers. Various ways to avoid bandits. Snake-proof hiking chaps. Automobiles that lightning can't spook and that zip us along paved routes full of food stores and restaurants.

How often do I pause to thank God for these blessings of ordinary life? Not often enough.

This chapter is titled "Thank God! Why?" I want in these pages to say that God is the ultimate giver of all that's good in our lives and therefore the fitting recipient of our thanks. We so often overlook this blessed fact and sail along oblivious to the blessed winds that are filling our sails.

Thankfulness for God's Good Creation

In 1883 we get not only the drama of the Duttons' odyssey across the plains but also the beauty of the plains themselves. They came to be called "plains" because they were plain. No hills, few trees, little water. What you mostly have on a plain is a broad, grassy flatland that seemingly goes on forever. So boring!

And yet. The plains have a kind of beauty that cinematographer Ben Richardson captures so splendidly in 1883 that if you freeze the frame almost anywhere in an episode the result belongs on a poster. You might get a breathtaking expanse of sky with the intriguing shapes of backlit clouds. Or, at night, the black dome stretching from horizon to horizon, lit by a yellow moon and an impossible wealth of diamond-like stars. Or the grassy land itself, its buffalo moving across it in stately herds and its tallgrass waving in the wind.

God's beauty is in the plains, as surely as in mountains and woods and seas.

In her Newbery Medal–winning book, *Sarah, Plain and Tall*,[5] Patricia MacLachlan tells the story of widower Jacob Witting on the prairie with his young son Caleb and daughter Anna. Jacob is lonely, so he does what other lonely widowers

Listen to Walt Whitman, one of America's most important poets: "As to scenery (giving my own thought and feeling), while I know the standard claim is that Yosemite, Niagara Falls, the Upper Yellowstone and the like afford the greatest natural shows, I am not so sure but the prairies and plains, while less stunning at first sight, last longer, fill the esthetic sense fuller, precede all the rest, and make North America's characteristic landscape."[a]

did in the late 1800s. He places an ad in the paper, hoping to attract a mail-order bride. Sarah Elisabeth Wheaton answers the ad and says she will come to Jacob by train. "I will wear a yellow bonnet," she says. "I am plain and tall."[6]

Sarah has spent her life by the sea in Maine. Knowing this, Caleb and Anna fear that the prairie will bore her. Anna worries that Sarah won't actually come to a land of "fields and grass and sky and not much else."[7] But Sarah does arrive in her yellow bonnet and makes a home with Jacob and Anna and Caleb—a home on the prairie with its red and orange Indian paintbrush, its goldenrod and wild asters and prairie violets. This is a land of meadowlarks and bobolinks and ring-necked pheasants. The prairie, seemingly so featureless, is alive with beauty.

And, remarkably, to Sarah "the land rolls a little like the sea."[8]

Creation is the masterpiece of God's artistry, and its richness a gift for our senses. I'm thinking right now of dewdrops that shine like jewels on blades of cool grass, peonies fragrant under a warming sun, the feel of a cool breeze on a summer day, the staccato rat-a-tat of woodpeckers answering each other across the woods outside my house, the taste of freshly caught salmon grilled over charcoal on a seaside beach.

If we love God's good creation, we will have limitless occasions to give God our thanks and to thrill a little at God's
ingenuity in fashioning it. When we Christians give thanks
for God's goodness, we often concentrate on God's grace for
us sinners. Of course. This is the heart of the biblical drama,
centering on the work of Jesus Christ, "who was handed over
to death for our trespasses and was raised for our justification" (Rom. 4:25).

But the biblical drama is three movements, not just two. The
drama is not just sin and grace, but creation, sin, and grace.
Creation is there first. Creation is what sin spoils. Creation is
the platform for the drama. In fact, some of the salvation in
which the psalmists rejoice tells of God restoring Israel's food
supply, her sowing and reaping:

> Those who go out weeping,
>   bearing the seed for sowing,
> shall come home with shouts of joy,
>   carrying their sheaves. (Ps. 126:6)

Count this verse as a mere warm-up for the rhapsody the
psalmists compose when they celebrate God's salvation for
them by providing the goodness of creation:

> You visit the earth and water it,
>   you greatly enrich it;
> the river of God is full of water;
>   you provide the people with grain,
>   for so you have prepared it.
> You water its furrows abundantly,
>   settling its ridges,
> softening it with showers,
>   and blessing its growth.

> You crown the year with your bounty;
> > your wagon tracks overflow with richness.
> The pastures of the wilderness overflow,
> > the hills gird themselves with joy,
> the meadows clothe themselves with flocks,
> > the valleys deck themselves with grain,
> > they shout and sing together for joy. (Ps. 65:9–13)[9]

This is an ecstasy of thanks, a festival of gratitude, with the psalmist's rhetoric soaring to match the surging enthusiasm of his heart. Here is creation thanksgiving in a full-throated cry, as buoyant and passionate as anything in Scripture.

Grace Is for Sinners but Many Churches Don't Like to Talk about It

In saying why it's *God* we humans need to thank, it's natural to start with such gifts as creation and ordinary life within it. It's then appropriate to go on to recount God's great redemptive gifts—the ones that forgive, liberate, and deliver us.

The chief of these is that God saves sinners. It sounds so simple. God saves sinners. But behind this simple sentence is a world of suffering—the suffering caused by human sin and the suffering of God in redeeming it.

None of us can doubt the suffering caused by sin. Kids bully other kids in school and mock them online. Men beat up women and then blame them for causing the beating: "You see what you made me do?" People of majority groups scorn people of minority groups and find ways to let them know it. Some employees lose their job not to automation or to out-sourcing or to necessary downsizing but to corporate politics driven by envy and greed. Heads of large nations cast their eye on the natural resources of small nations and devise ways to plunder them.

You could add countless examples of your own.

And yet, in recent decades many of us have not heard much about sin, even in church. Catholics, Lutherans, and Episcopalians still have rites for confession of sin. But in very many evangelical churches these days, sin is a rare topic.

Here's a telling fact. Christian Copyright Licensing International (CCLI) is an organization that licenses songs and hymns to 250,000 churches in North America on a subscription basis so that they don't have to apply for copyright every time they want to put the words of a song or a hymn on a screen. With CCLI they can pay a fee on a subscription basis and then show the songs and hymns.

Many of these songs and hymns are contemporary compositions for use in contemporary worship—and, as you may know, contemporary worship in evangelical Protestant churches for the last few decades has consisted in especially three things: praise songs followed by a number of quieter worship songs—so-called praise and worship. Then comes the teaching or sermon. Unlike Catholic, Lutheran, and Episcopal liturgies, contemporary worship typically includes no penitence at all. If you examine the content of the most popular songs used in churches with subscriptions to CCLI, you will find very, very few penitential songs.

We may speculate about the reasons for this amazing development in evangelical churches. Surely one reason is that evangelical churches are set up to grow. They want to be seeker-friendly. Mindful that seekers come to church from a no-fault American culture in which tolerance is the big virtue and intolerance the big vice, worship planners in evangelical churches often want nothing in the service that sounds judgmental. And so lots of evangelical church services these days are almost unrelievedly cheerful. Where sin is concerned, not a discouraging word is heard.

Here we have an obvious problem. Evangelical worship that is emptied of sorrow over sin makes thanksgiving for God's grace just baffling. Grace is God's unmerited favor for *sinners*, for people who grieve God, offend others, and sully themselves. Grace for people who tell damaging lies. Grace for people who neglect their aging parents. Grace for people who cheat on their taxes, cheat on their spouses, cheat on their résumé. And this is only the beginning of the list of sins we human beings commit every day.

How do we thank God for forgiving our sin when we won't talk about sin? How would that go? "Amazing Grace" is the all-time most popular Christian hymn, and it has me confess that such grace is for "a wretch like me." How could this classic hymn fit in churches that throw a furniture blanket over the topic of sin and move it out of the sanctuary?

Just what is the topic many churches want to banish? God saves sinners. That's what needs to be hushed up.

But the writers of the Bible never knew that it was necessary to hush up this fact. They keep repeating that God saves sinners.

- "Christ Jesus came into the world to save sinners—of whom I am the foremost." (1 Tim. 1:15)
- "God proves his love for us in that while we still were sinners Christ died for us." (Rom. 5:8)
- "The wages of sin is death, but the free gift of God is eternal life in Christ Jesus our Lord." (Rom. 6:23)

In faithful Christian churches, this is the central message. Nothing obscures it. Nothing interferes with it. Nothing supersedes it. What follows this message is our full, hearty, sincere thanks. We thank God not only for the forgiveness of our sins but also for God's mercy that comforts and heals us when we are the victims of other people's sins. This ministry of mercy is a major dimension of God's grace. Maybe the minister is silent about sin, but people in the congregation are meanwhile comforting each other, embracing each other, weeping with each other over the suffering caused by sin.

Grace for sinners. It's important to understand that God's grace is not tolerant. God is not soft on sin. God hates sin, judges sin, condemns sin. It's striking to me that God hates sin so much that God is always trying to get it out of sight, out of mind, out of the way. God can't stand sin. God covers it, forgets it, washes it away, sweeps it away, buries it in the heart of the sea (Ps. 32:1; Jer. 31:34; 1 John 1:9; Isa. 44:22; Mic. 7:19).

God will not tolerate sin, but God will forgive it so that it's out of sight, out of mind, out of the way, and can't come between God and the people whom God loves.

Grace Is Powerful, Expensive, Lavish, Surprising

To remove sin, God regenerates our dead hearts so we're willing to confess our sins and seek God's forgiveness. This is grace more powerful than we could ever imagine.

The Canons of Dort tell us that the Holy Spirit's regeneration of a human heart is not "inferior in power to that of creation." God's grace *overpowers* sin. God doesn't just excuse it. Surely God doesn't just prettify or embellish it. God's grace is not a mere grace *note*. It's a power that revives the dead. The grace of God works on people who are lousy patients—people who resist and resent any interference with them. Grace is tough love that remakes people in spite of themselves. Grace has the power, C. S. Lewis testifies, to drag people kicking and screaming into the kingdom of God:

> The Prodigal Son at least walked home on his own feet. But who can duly adore that Love which will open the high gates to a prodigal who is brought in kicking, struggling, resentful, and darting his eyes in every direction for a chance of escape?[10]

Grace is for wretches who really aren't up for getting saved. And it is still grace even when its muscles are flexed and its energy is rubbing our fur the wrong way. We want to be stroked, but God's grace comes to save. It is more stubborn than our sin. That is reason enough to exult over it in our thanksgiving.

Let me add that grace is free but not cheap. The grace of Jesus Christ is held out to us in wounded hands. We know how it hurts to accept an injury without retaliating. How much more the Son of God, who absorbed the sin of the whole world into himself without passing it back and so cut an otherwise

The Spirit of God "penetrates into our inmost being, opens the closed heart, softens the hard heart, and . . . infuses new qualities into the will, making the dead will alive, the evil one good, the unwilling one willing, and the stubborn one compliant. . . . This is the regeneration . . . that God works in us without our help . . . a marvelous, hidden, and inexpressible work, which is not lesser than or inferior in power to that of creation or raising the dead."

—Canons of Dort[b]

endless loop of vengeance. Grace is graciously given, but it is expensive and it always comes to us with blood on it.

And this is another cause for thanks.

Grace is powerful. It's expensive. It's also lavish, profuse, uncalculating. The source of grace is not a small pipe with a thin stream but a huge fountain that sprays high and wide in every direction. John's Gospel says that Jesus Christ came to us *full* of grace and truth and that he has poured it out on us as "grace upon grace" (John 1:14, 16).

The grace of God in Jesus Christ is full, lavish, profuse. Yes, the Christian church has traditionally said that God's grace in the end is only for some and that all others are eternally lost. The church has cited Scriptures to support this painful idea. Accordingly, across the centuries, faithful Christians have agonized over their unbelieving loved ones. Are they bound for eternal torment in hell? Knowing this, how could I ever enjoy eternal life?

Some Scriptures do seem restrictive. But other Scriptures are full of seemingly boundless grace:

- "Just as [Adam's] trespass led to condemnation for all, so [Jesus Christ's] act of righteousness leads to justification and life *for all.*" (Rom. 5:18)
- "In [Christ] all the fullness of God was pleased to dwell, and through him God was pleased to reconcile to himself *all things*, whether on earth or in heaven, by making peace through the blood of his cross." (Col. 1:19–20)
- "Jesus Christ the righteous . . . is the atoning sacrifice for our sins, and not for ours only but also for the sins of *the whole world.*" (1 John 2:1–2)

These are not the dreamy wishes of sentimental universalists. These are the strong, confident declarations of the Word of God.

Grace is uncalculating. In Jesus's parable of the lost sheep, a shepherd leaves ninety-nine sheep unprotected to go out after one that has strayed (Luke 15:3–4). Maybe not wise, but gracious. In Jesus's parable of the workers in the vineyard, an employer pays latecomers just as much as those who have labored from the crack of dawn through the midday heat (Matt. 20:1–16). Not good labor policy, but profusely gracious. In Jesus's parable of the prodigal son, a father waits outside his home, peering down the road that winds in from a far country, straining his eyes toward the familiar profile, the familiar gait of his prodigal son (Luke 15:11–32). The son has a memorized confession he wants to make, but the father doesn't focus on anything like *that*! He runs out to meet his son, hugging him and shouting for somebody to pour drinks and strike up the band. His son had been rebellious and disrespectful, but none of that matters now. All that matters is that his son who was lost has now been found and is safely at home.

Lavish, heedless, amazing grace. Not a trickle but a flood tide. And an occasion for ceaseless thanks to God.

Grace is also surprising. The prodigal son expects a lecture and gets a hug. The workers in the vineyard expect short wages and are paid in full. The disciple Peter, who had denied his Lord, almost certainly expected a rebuke for it. What he gets is a special announcement of his Lord's resurrection, addressed just to him.

To me this is one of the most moving stories of grace in all the Bible. As Mark tells it, three frightened women who love Jesus go to his tomb on Easter morning. They are carrying spices because the only thing they can still do for Jesus now is to keep his death from smelling like death. At his tomb they are startled to encounter "a young man, dressed in a white robe." What he says is stunning: "Do not be alarmed. . . . He has been raised; he is not here. . . . Go, tell his disciples and Peter" (Mark 16:5–7).

And Peter! Why is the world's best news especially for Peter? Because he's guilty and feeling guilty. Because he thinks he's no longer a disciple. Because he fears that his denial of Jesus has made him forever an outcast.

But, no! Astonishingly, no! "Go, tell his disciples and Peter."

Thank God! Why? We know why. God is the God of goodness in ordinary life, of wonders in creation, and of amazing grace for people like Peter and people like us.

7

It Could Always Be Worse

We encounter God's goodness in ordinary life all the time and should be grateful for it. In the example from the previous chapter, the Mexican fisherman's life was blessed by his kids and his siestas with his wife and his music-making buddies. We also saw in the previous chapter that we meet God's goodness in the wonders of creation, which enchant us with their beauty and feed us with their bounties. Think of wheat fields with their amber waves of grain and of freestone streams with their high-leaping rainbow trout. Finally, detailing the various riches of God's grace, I said that we should give thanks that it saves sinners—even sinners like Peter who shun their Savior.

But, of course, a moment's thought disturbs this inspiring picture. Look around the world. Yes, you will see plenty of people enjoying the benefits of ordinary life. But also plenty of people with lousy daily lives. Maybe they are squeezed by poverty or by a merciless government. Maybe prolonged drought and famine make the wonders of God's creation less wonderful in their region. Maybe they can't hear the gospel of salvation for sinners because they are too depressed to listen.

And these are just some of the adversities God's human creatures face every day.

So what becomes of our gratitude when life hurts? Does gratitude make any sense? Are we clinging to some fantasy of God's goodness when all around us we see life's badness? God's providence is supposed to *provide* for us. But what if it doesn't?

This problem looms so large in the history of faith that we can't evade it. No doubt it ranks as *the* largest problem in the history of faith. And it has no simple or obvious solution.

So how do we cope? In this chapter I'm going to suggest a strategy that belongs both to the biblical witness and to general human wisdom. It has to do with frankly acknowledging obvious trouble but refusing to concede that trouble has the last word.

Let's start with a famous old story.

The Poor Man in His Crowded Hut

A Yiddish folktale tells of a poor man whose one-room hut is too small for his big family. The story is titled "It Could Always Be Worse," and it is unforgettable.[1] The poor man has not only his wife, himself, and their six children living in their tiny home, but also his mother. It's too much. They are crammed together, getting in each other's way and squabbling over small matters. The kids cry a lot—especially on winter days when everybody must stay indoors because it's too cold to be out.

At his wit's end, the poor man appeals to his rabbi. Old and wise, the rabbi gives his mind to the man's predicament, pulling on his beard as he thinks. Finally he says, "Do you have animals, maybe a couple of chickens?"

The man says, "O yes, two hens plus a rooster and a goose."

"Fine," says the rabbi. "Bring them inside the hut."

The man is surprised at this strange advice but does as the rabbi says, pulling his birds indoors. Things, of course, get worse, what with all the clucking and crowing and the feathers in the family's soup.

So the poor man returns to the rabbi and tells him of the growing chaos in the hut. The rabbi thinks some more and says, "Is it possible that you have a goat?"

"Yes," says the man. "I'm very poor, but I do have a goat."

"Bring it inside," says the rabbi.

The man questions the wisdom of adding another animal to the mix, but he does what the rabbi says. Things are now even worse. The goat adds its bleating to all the noise and it butts everybody.

The man returns to his rabbi and says, "I can't take it anymore. The noise and crowding and butting are driving us crazy."

Always thoughtful, the rabbi asks, "Any chance you have a cow? Maybe a young one? Maybe an old one? It doesn't matter."

The poor man objects, "Oh, no! You can't be serious."

"Get that cow indoors at once," says the rabbi.

Now life in the hut is impossible. The cow takes up so much space and makes so much noise and produces so many cow pies. Besides, it tramples the children's toys.

Desperate, the poor man returns to his rabbi and says that life in the hut is a nightmare. Pondering the matter a last time, and speaking with a kind voice, the rabbi says, "Go home, my good man, and let all the animals out of the hut."

Doing as he is told, the man finds that the nightmare is over and that peace has descended on his tiny home. No more crowing or bleating or mooing. No more crowding or butting or trampling. No more cow pies. The man and his family now sleep soundly, breathe easily, and enjoy life in their cozy hut.

It could always be worse! This observation has become a staple of general human wisdom, expressed in proverbs from many times and places:

> "Half a loaf is better than none."
> "The smallest fish is better than an empty dish."
> "Better a bush than an open field" (when hunting for shelter).[2]

Poet Robert Bly tells about his mother, who had a particular variant of the "it could always be worse" strategy. He would scrape his knee as a kid and bring the injury to his mother. As she treated it she'd say, "Just be thankful you didn't break your leg." Bly says it drove him nuts at the time. Later, he saw its "perverse wisdom."[3]

Choosing to Focus on the Good

The point is that we have an option when it comes to assessing our situation. We can admit that it's not ideal, but then deliberately focus on whatever might be good inside it. For any of us who prize gratitude, this is a life strategy. We can go through life finding *something* to be thankful for, no matter whatever else is wrong. And it's available to us in a host of ordinary circumstances.

In a Thanksgiving sermon Jeff Chapman illustrates the strategy:

- I'm not thankful for the mess I have to clean up after Thanksgiving dinner. But I am thankful because the mess means I have just been surrounded by great friends and family.
- I'm not thankful for the taxes I have to pay. But I am thankful because the taxes mean I have been employed this year.
- I'm not thankful for the lawn that needs mowing, the windows that need cleaning, and the gutters that need fixing. But I am thankful because the housework means I have a place to call home.
- I'm not thankful that the only spot in the busy parking lot is at the far end. But I am thankful that I am capable of walking that distance.
- I'm not thankful for the off-key voice of the lady who sings behind me in church. But, considering the alternative, I am thankful that I can, at least, hear.[4]

"Considering the alternative." So much of gratitude rests on this simple strategy. We choose to find the good inside an otherwise unsatisfying situation by considering the alternative. "Considering the alternative" is, of course, just another way of saying, "It could always be worse." In our Yiddish folktale, the poor man in his tiny hut focuses exclusively on his cramped condition. His rabbi, rich in wisdom, devises a strategy to help the poor man consider the alternative.

When it comes to considering the alternative as a way of triggering our gratitude for ordinary things in daily life, I prize a TED Talk Hans Rosling once gave.[5] Rosling was a Swedish

Matthew Henry (1662–1714), a noted British preacher and Bible commentator, was confronted and robbed in London. He had a remarkable perspective on the event: "Let me be thankful, first, because I was never robbed before; second, because although they took my purse, they did not take my life; third, because although they took my all, it was not much; and fourth, because it was I who was robbed, not I who robbed."[a]

physician, professor, inventor, champion statistician, master communicator, humanitarian—and much else. In the talk I have in mind, Rosling tells of what happened when his family first came to own a washing machine when he was a boy of about four in Sweden.

His father and mother had been saving up for years to buy it. When the machine arrived, his mother loaded it and his grandmother asked to be the one to push the start button. She was excited because she had heated water over a wood fire and hand-washed clothes for seven children and could hardly imagine the convenience of having an electrical machine do the work instead.

After starting the machine, Rosling's grandmother pulled up a chair so she could sit directly in front of the washer and watch the action through the window in its door. Mesmerized, she watched the machine wash through a whole cycle. She was transfixed.

Commenting on this boyhood memory, Rosling says his grandmother's amazement sticks with him. In the developed world, we smile at this story. But in the rest of the world, people would completely understand Rosling's grandmother. Only about two billion out of seven billion people in the world wash their clothes by machine. The rest (almost invariably women) wash by hand. They have to find wood, build a fire, and heat water they have carried home. Or they must tote their laundry to a stream at some distance to wash their clothes with a scrub board. It's hard, time-consuming work either way, and it needs to be done every week.

The washing machine in his own home was magical, says Rosling. While it cleaned the family's clothes, his mother didn't have to. She could walk to the library, borrow books, and read to little Hans, starting him on the road to all the things he would become.

There's a Blessing in This Somewhere

Until I listened to Rosling's TED Talk, it never occurred to me to include my washing machine in my daily prayers of gratitude. It never occurred to me to dwell on the blessing of a washer and dryer. I took them for granted because *I never considered the alternative.* I wasn't properly grateful for them. You could surely add examples of your own. Suppose you have a refrigerator. What would be the alternative? How would you preserve perishable food? Suppose you have a stove and an oven. When it comes to cooking, what would be the alternative? Suppose you have a furnace. How else would you heat your whole house?

Choosing to focus on the good inside a bad situation is a strategy that requires a certain outlook on life, a certain perspective. If I have this strategy, I never completely resign myself to an unhappy state of affairs. I always look for the ray of sunshine that has gotten through the clouds.

"Let us try to see things from their better side: You complain about seeing thorny rose bushes; I rejoice and give thanks to the gods that thorns have roses."

—Alphonse Karr[b]

In 2004 Marilynne Robinson published *Gilead,* a novel that won her a Pulitzer Prize. In it she tells the story of an elderly small-town minister, John Ames. He's intelligent, devout, and—for most of his life—lonely. He was born around 1900, so his ancestors are nineteenth-century people. He recalls a family story about his grandfather. When "someone remarked in his hearing that he had lost an eye in the Civil War, he said, 'I prefer to remember that I have kept one.'"[6]

Ames tells of his mother in her kitchen listening to a storm lashing their house with wind and rain. Suddenly she remembered that her wash was on the line—the wash she had spent hours doing by hand—and exclaimed to her son about what the storm must be doing to it: "Those sheets must be so heavy that they're dragging in the mud, if they haven't pulled the lines down altogether." Then, closing one eye, Ames's mother looked at him and said, "I know there is a blessing in this somewhere."[7]

But is knowing "there is a blessing in this somewhere" unrealistic—just a sunny-side-up fiction from a novel?

I don't think so.

In a perceptive book titled *Thanks!,* Robert Emmons adds to our knowledge of real-life instances in which people confronted by distressing circumstances nonetheless find something to be grateful for.[8] Emmons found that lots of people with debilitating diseases still believe themselves to be blessed. It's as if their disease, with its deprivations, has made them exquisitely sensitive to the offsetting blessings they enjoy despite all. He adds that the same is true for the people who care for them. One example: it's tough to be a caregiver for someone with Alzheimer's. Caregivers have to seize hold of small things to be grateful for: "Bill called me by my name." "Bill remembered that it was July, not January."[9]

Could there possibly be a blessing in this somewhere? Emmons notes that in the weeks and months following 9/11, Americans reported an elevated sense of gratitude for their loved ones, their friends—for life itself.[10]

Thinking of historical figures who rejoiced in the midst of awful circumstances, Emmons cites St. Paul, Dietrich Bonhoeffer, Corrie ten Boom, and Horatio Spafford, who wrote the consoling hymn "It Is Well with My Soul" after losing four daughters to an accident at sea.[11]

Of these, let's consider the life of the apostle Paul as recounted in Scripture. He endured a lifetime of suffering that would make most of us whimper and beg for relief if exposed to it for even a day. Paul was beaten, stoned, and shipwrecked. He was in danger from rivers, danger from robbers, danger in the city, danger in the wilderness. He was hungry, cold, and naked under the lash. He was jailed (2 Cor. 11:24–27). Still, while up to his neck in trouble—and sometimes from prison— Paul pours out gratitude for God's grace, for triumph over the forces of evil, for his friends in the churches he founded.

His thanksgiving is full-throated and joyous:

- "Thanks be to God, who gives us the victory through our Lord Jesus Christ." (1 Cor. 15:57)

- "Thanks be to God for his indescribable gift." (2 Cor. 9:15)
- "Blessed be the God and Father of our Lord Jesus Christ, who has blessed us in Christ with every spiritual blessing in the heavenly places." (Eph. 1:3)
- "I thank my God through Jesus Christ for all of you [Roman Christians], because your faith is proclaimed throughout the world." (Rom. 1:8)

Remarkable! And, shorn of its coat of familiarity, deeply inspiring! Paul was gripped by the magnificence of God's power and love to such a degree that his sufferings seemed to him trivial, irrelevant, almost uninteresting.

Where would he have learned to look at life like this? What in his background might have given him an example to follow?

Lament and Faith

Paul was a learned Jew. He knew the Hebrew Scriptures. He knew the psalms, with all their laments over the troubles suffered by the people of God. He also knew that the psalms of lament, almost without exception, conclude in faith. In fact, many of the psalms conclude with vows of praise and thanksgiving for God's redemptive love.

This is a great consolation for us believers. If you doubt God's providence amid overwhelming distress, then the Bible is your book. Its psalms, so often read for their praise and thanksgiving, are also full of lament over the world's evil. In fact, two-thirds of the psalms call God's attention to what's wrong. Your enemies are attacking! I'm hurting! You aren't helping! You're not even paying attention!

The psalmists do have faith. Else they wouldn't bother with God at all. But their faith takes the form of lament. Sometimes it takes the form of complaint. Occasionally the complaints sound almost like accusations:

- "Why, O LORD, do you stand far off? Why do you hide yourself in times of trouble?" (Ps. 10:1)
- "How long, O LORD? Will you forget me forever?" (Ps. 13:1)
- "My God, my God, why have you forsaken me?" (Ps. 22:1)[12]

I'll repeat that the psalmists are *believers*. They know all about God's righteousness, and they trust it. That's exactly why they are so full of consternation. It seems to them that something has gone wrong with God. Some wire has gotten crossed in God. God isn't acting in character. The psalmists are baffled and upset because they think God has somehow forgotten how to be God. So they try, you might say, to *activate* God, or even to wake God up:

- "Rise up, O LORD! Deliver me, O my God!" (Ps. 3:7)
- "Rise up, O LORD, in your anger; lift yourself up against the fury of my enemies." (Ps. 7:6)
- "Rouse yourself! Why do you sleep, O Lord? Awake!" (Ps. 44:23)

A psalmist dares to do some straight talking to God because he trusts that God can take it. God can absorb it and still love him. In fact, the psalmist trusts God to answer with a word of peace or reassurance. He dares to complain to God and to try to stir God up to action because Israel has a history with God. Didn't God lead them out of the land of Egypt, out of the house of bondage? Will God not do mighty work once again?

Psalm 22 begins with an abject lament ("My God, my God, why have you forsaken me?") but then goes on to recall that Israel's ancestors trusted God to deliver them and God came through for them. In fact, says the psalmist, God has come through for me too: "He did not hide his face from me, but heard when I cried to him" (v. 24). Near the end of the psalm, the psalmist says simply, "I shall live for him" (v. 29).

Psalm 13 deplores God's absence: "How long, O LORD? . . . How long will you hide your face from me?" (v. 1). But the psalmist ends by saying, "My heart shall rejoice in your salvation" (v. 5).

The author of Psalm 42 laments that "my tears have been my food day and night, while people say to me continually, 'Where is your God?'" (v. 3). But the psalmist famously ends his lament by arguing with himself:

> Why are you cast down, O my soul,
> and why are you disquieted within me?
> Hope in God; for I shall again praise him,
> my help and my God. (v. 11)

God Is Not Aloof

In the psalms of lament, St. Paul could find inspiration for his own faith in times of trouble. He was beaten, persecuted, and harassed, but not crushed. He saw himself carrying in his own body the death of Jesus—in a way that would also make visible the life of Jesus (2 Cor. 4:8–10). Paul knew that when it comes to finding God's good inside our evil, the real test is the suffering and death of Jesus, climaxing in Jesus's own lament.

Nailed to his cross, Jesus cries out in agony, "My God, my God, why have you forsaken me?" (Mark 15:34, using the lament of Ps. 22). By doing so, he was taking his place alongside other Jewish martyrs of the first century who used these same words as they died.[13]

It's important to see that Jesus's pain was unimaginably more than physical. He was feeling the cold chill of abandonment by his beloved Father at the very moment when he most needed his Father's strength. Other martyrs were crucified. Other martyrs felt abandoned by God. But none of them were at the same time struggling—all alone—to absorb a whole world's evil into themselves.

The scene on Golgotha tells us how fearful a thing atonement is, even for the Son of God. All his securities had been stripped away, including his clothing. Mark tells us that

> priests had plotted against him,
> Judas had betrayed him,
> three disciples fell asleep on him,
> witnesses lied about him,
> and Peter denied him.[14]

Each was a stake in his heart, long before the Romans drove them through his hands and feet.

Mark tells us that Pilate flogged Jesus and soldiers mocked him. When the soldiers got tired of kneeling in front of Jesus and then belting him in the face, they led him out to crucify him (Mark 15:16–20). All these assaults on a human spirit, all these terrible degradations of Jesus's dignity kept on till finally he was led to the cross. Mark is telling us, I think, that where

103

mockery is concerned, crucifixion is just a way of finishing it off.

"My God, my God, why have you forsaken me?" The words carry not just a tone of loneliness but something more horrible than that, something like a sense of astonishment! There's astonishment in Jesus's words, as if he never expected the abyss to be this deep. He never expected to find God's back turned on him. Maybe, as in much lament, there is even a hint of accusation in Jesus's words.

And yet John's Gospel reports that they weren't his last words. At the end Jesus says, "It is finished" (19:30), which in the world of the Fourth Gospel means that he has achieved what he came to do—to act as "the Lamb of God who takes away the sin of the world" (1:29). Luke reports that Jesus's last words were, "Father, into your hands I commend my spirit," and that Jesus was "crying with a loud voice" as he said the words (23:46). Mark says the same about Jesus's cry of abandonment: "Jesus cried out with a loud voice, 'My God, my God, why have you forsaken me?'" (15:34).

I find the combination of these reports stirring. A loud lament. An equally loud declaration of faith. May we not follow our Savior in this—deploring the worst with everything we have but also proclaiming our faith with everything we have?

Despair is never the believer's last word. The last word, even as we face Jesus's death, is a word of faith. We praise God's love. We pour out a heart full of thanks that our Savior was willing to die for us.

Here is the ultimate case of finding light in darkness. Here is the prime example of choosing to focus on goodness that lies inside evil. Jesus's crucifixion was a horrible injustice perpetrated on him by wicked men. We deplore it with everything we have. But we Christians choose to focus instead on the fact that in Jesus's suffering and death we can see that God is not aloof. God is not exempt. In Jesus's suffering God shares our lot and can therefore be trusted. We find gospel consolation in Jesus's sorrow because he was bearing *our* griefs and carrying *our* sorrows. He was bearing them when he shouted at heaven. He was carrying them when he beat at the heart of God. This is our faith in the God who is not aloof. And we say so with everything we have.

Someone once said that if God's love were available only to those who were sure of what God was up to, most of us would be priced out of the market. We're short on answers to suffering. We don't understand a lot of what happens in the world. We don't know why God permits so much pain in the same world that God loves.

But we do know this: We have a suffering Lord, Jesus Christ, the righteous one. He shared our lot, accepting the worst of our suffering and showing that it is safe for us to trust the God we often do not understand.

8

Savoring and Celebrating

Let's get our bearings. So far, we've seen what gratitude is, how we get it, what keeps us from getting it, what happens to us if we get it, how the Bible treats it, and why God, in particular, deserves our thanks.

In the previous chapter, I started talking about how grateful people live. We gratefully home in on the good in bad situations, often by considering the alternative. In this chapter I'll say that grateful people make a habit of savoring and celebrating good things. In the next chapter I'll add that grateful people take care of things they're thankful for and that they make good deeds their "central business" to show gratitude to God for their salvation.

Thanks a Thousand

Savoring. To start our thinking about this appealing topic, let's consider a popular pleasure. Many of us enjoy drinking a cup of coffee, especially in the morning. Most coffee contains caffeine, of course, and caffeine stimulates our central nervous system just enough to get us going. But there are other benefits too. Freshly brewed coffee smells good and tastes good. We pour our coffee and appreciate its rich, dark color. We drink our coffee hot, which is a comfort to us. Its heat makes us sip it—which places our face over the cup long enough to enjoy its aroma. (In some cultures people savor coffee by slurping it.) The ritual of drinking coffee in the morning also signals that a new day has begun and that we need to get with its program. That's why advice columnists sometimes say to clueless correspondents, "Wake up and smell the coffee!"

Writer A. J. Jacobs was sipping his morning joe one day and letting his mind wander along the chain of people who had to do their job for that steaming cup to get into his hands. It turned out to be a very long chain—thousands of people—and, remarkably, Jacobs decided he needed somehow to thank them all. And to write a book about his journey to do so.[1]

The journey begins in his local coffee shop, Joe Coffee, with his barista. He thanks her as she tells him how grateful she is when customers make eye contact with her and don't just growl their order while looking at their phone. He arranges to meet the head buyer and taster for the Joe Coffee Company and thanks him. He calls up the inventor of the special lid on the cups used by Joe Coffee and thanks him. (The lid is designed for releasing aroma and for easy sipping.) He calls up the maker of the Java Jacket—the sleeve on cups that keeps you from burning your fingers—and thanks her. He thanks people who roast beans for Joe Coffee as well as people who weigh and bag the beans. He drives into the Catskills and thanks people there who send fresh, good-tasting water to

New York City for use in coffee making. He even travels to South America to thank Colombian farmers for growing the beans that the Joe Coffee Company will crush to make Jacobs's coffee taste and smell good every morning.

Along the way, Jacobs ponders the vast web of dependence we all live in. We depend on others for virtually everything we eat and drink, and we seldom pause to give thanks for them. As for our morning coffee, it gets to us in part because of all the people who use "motorcycles, trucks, boats, vans, pallets, shoulders, and forklifts."[2] Almost everything we buy in a store has been delivered there by a truck driver. Almost everything in a warehouse (think 150-pound bags of coffee beans) had to be forklifted into place on pallets.[3] And somebody had to make the pallets. Somebody had to drive the forklifts that moved them.

I live—we all live—in a great web of dependence. When I give thanks for my breakfast coffee, I now try to remember this blessed web and give thanks for the people in it. I can't thank them directly, but I can thank their Creator. And I can let all this help me savor my morning coffee.

The Virtuous Cycle

Grateful people *savor* good things. They receive these things as gifts, paying full attention to them and taking their time with them. They savor a good book enough to feel bad when they turn its last page. They savor their favorite music enough to play it repeatedly. They savor quiet time, sex, beauty in nature. They take photos so they can preserve a good memory and enjoy it at their leisure. They dwell in the present with good things, surrounding them with awareness and lingering over them. They dream of wonderful things in the future, anticipating and yearning for them. They purposely spend time outdoors so they can watch cattails sway, hear birds sing, smell blooming lilacs.

Savoring is part of a "virtuous cycle." We all know what's meant by a vicious cycle. It's a sequence of actions in lockstep that aggravate each other to make a situation worse and worse. An alcoholic gets drunk and hungover. To relieve the hangover, he gets drunk and has another hangover. This makes him want a drink. And so on. He relieves distress with the same thing that caused it in a continuous downward spiral. It's a classic vicious cycle.

But gratitude and savoring are part of a virtuous cycle. In this cycle a grateful person receives good things and is already inclined to savor them. She lives expectantly, appreciatively. She sees so many things in life as gifts. And, significantly, she pays close attention to them.

Suppose, for example, that her beloved husband cooks and plates a meal for her. In her appreciative frame of mind, she would never treat it as mere fuel. She would never just shovel it in while playing a game on her handheld device. No, she receives her plate with full awareness. She registers that it's a gift from her beloved and lets this warm her heart. She focuses on her plate and brings all her senses to it. She breathes the aroma of sautéed garlic. She lets her eyes linger on the green, red, and golden-brown colors on her plate. When she cuts into a roasted brussels sprout, she delights that it's still partly crisp. When she picks up a deviled egg, she loves its smooth, almost slippery feel.

Tasting her food, she takes small bites and takes time with each one. She doesn't dawdle or let her food get cold, but she

> "Our holiday food splurge was a small crate of tangerines, which we found ridiculously thrilling after an eight-month abstinence from citrus. . . . Lily hugged each one to her chest before undressing it as gently as a doll. Watching her do that as she sat cross-legged on the floor one morning in pink pajamas, with bliss lighting her cheeks, I thought: Lucky is the world, to receive this grateful child."
>
> —Barbara Kingsolver[a]

doesn't gobble either. She eats deliberately. She gives her taste buds time to work their magic and bring her joy. She registers the size and texture of her bites. She crunches crisp food. She squeezes and swallows the juice of juicy foods. She's mindful of saltiness, sweetness, slight bitterness.

In a word, she *savors* her food. In the virtuous cycle of gratitude and savoring, her thankful outlook on life makes her inclined to savor good things. And savoring them makes her all the more thankful for them.

Grateful people savor their good things. They focus attention on them, take time over them, engage all their senses to enjoy them. They immerse themselves in their enjoyment of them. Like A. J. Jacobs, if we are grateful we will also think for a moment about the blessed web of dependence we live in, and about the host of workers who had to do their job to bring us what we are now savoring.

Solomon Schimmel adds another way to savor. He recounts that in some documents of Judaism, God's "countless millions of favors" may be illustrated by rain. To a parched earth *each drop* of rain is a gift to be thankful for. It's not just "raining" outdoors. No, the heavens have been opened to release millions of distinct droplets, each targeting a distinct speck of dust.[4]

Another habit of rabbis, says Schimmel, is to formulate thanks to God for our food, but not just in general ("Thank you for our food"). No, there must be specific thanks for each fruit, each vegetable, each slice of bread that we are about to enjoy. The idea is that the pleasures to be derived from distinct foods and drinks are themselves distinct and thus deserve specific thanks![5]

Imagine parts of the world where families still sit around a table and eat dinner together. A mom or a dad leads the family in a prayer of thanks before anybody digs in. Imagine that it sounds like this: "Gracious God, you have provided these foods to nourish our bodies. Thank you for these eggs with their abundant protein that gives us energy and helps us heal. Thank you for these sweet potatoes with their carbohydrates that feed our brains and protect us against disease. Thank you for this fish and its good fats that build our cells and give us energy. Thank you for these tomatoes with their multiple vitamins that make our cells healthy. Thank you for this spinach with its minerals that strengthen our teeth and bones. Thank you for this juice that flushes poisons out of our bodies."

Unrealistic? Maybe. But what if a parent introduced the foods and their benefits to the table before the prayer and *then* said, "Let's thank God for our food!"

Children would never forget a scenario like this. Years later, even if they didn't reproduce it in their own families, they might still recall for their kids how table prayers went when they were growing up at home.

Raising Our Voices to Celebrate

Psalms are famous for their expressions of praise and thanksgiving. They praise God for a mighty deliverance, and they also thank God for it. They praise God for gracious love, and they also thank God for it. God is the ultimate giver behind all good things, and psalmists constantly say so.

What's more, they don't do it alone. Their gratitude isn't complete until they call others to praise and thank God *with* them. Not just other Israelites but all the nations. Not just the nations but also rivers and oceans and mountains. Psalmists in their exultation cannot fling their imagination wide enough to summon all creation to praise and thank God.

Psalm 98, for example, gives us these rollicking verses:

> Sing to the LORD a new song,
>> for he has done marvelous things;
> his right hand and his holy arm
>> have worked salvation for him. . . .
>
> Shout for joy to the LORD, all the earth,
>> burst into jubilant song with music;
> make music to the LORD with the harp,
>> with the harp and the sound of singing,
> with trumpets and the blast of the ram's horn—
>> shout for joy before the LORD, the King.
>
> Let the sea resound, and everything in it,
>> the world, and all who live in it.
> Let the rivers clap their hands,
>> let the mountains sing together for joy;
> let them sing before the LORD,
>> for he comes to judge the earth.
> He will judge the world in righteousness
>> and the peoples with equity. (vv. 1, 4–9 NIV)

This wonderful psalm has great centrifugal energy. The psalmist begins by calling to his first audience—probably temple worshipers—"Sing to the LORD a new song." Then he calls to all the peoples of the earth: "Shout for joy to the LORD, all the earth, . . . make music to the LORD." Then he calls God's creation to join the celebration of God's reign: "Let the sea resound. . . . Let the rivers clap their hands, let the mountains sing together for joy."

To think of everything—all peoples, places, and things—singing and shouting for joy to the Lord is, to me, an extraordinary thought and a true anticipation of the wonders in the full coming of the kingdom of God at the end of time. We will then have eternal delights marked by music and acclamation as people and all nature sing and ring with joy. Even the rivers and mountains, even the wolves and lambs, will play their part in celebrating the triumph of God, each in their own particular way. I can imagine whales breaching, elephants trumpeting, lions roaring, horses whinnying—all creatures great and small adding their unique voices to the chorus of joy.

We see in Psalm 98 exultant celebration. Celebration is more extravagant than savoring. Savoring and celebrating do partly overlap. In both, we focus our awareness on something good. We engage all our senses to enjoy it. We enjoy the details of what we love. Both savoring and celebrating express our gratitude for the gift in front of us and then *increase* our gratitude for it. This is the virtuous cycle we've been noticing. And, as we've seen, gratitude is the single best predictor of human well-being.

Savoring and celebrating do overlap. But celebration adds drama. In celebration we don't simply enjoy a good thing. We make a fuss over it. We get excited about it. We call other people's attention to it. We raise our voices over it. "Shout for joy to the LORD," Psalm 98 says.

Shouts well up from strong and joyful emotion. In celebration, there's no doubt that our shouts are shouts of joy. Think of soccer fans celebrating a goal or baseball fans celebrating a home run. Lots of shouting.

What else? In celebrations we raise our voices not just to shout but also to sing. "Burst into jubilant song with music," Psalm 98 says. When people celebrate, they want to sing. Football fans at a college game sing the school's fight song. Americans sing their national anthem before baseball games— a tradition that gained enormous momentum during the two world wars as patriotic feeling ran high.

In many countries, people sing at birthday parties. In the United States since about 1912 the song has been "Happy Birthday to You." People of other countries sing it too (it's been translated into eighteen languages),[6] or they sing their own birthday songs. In Mexico, for instance, people sing "Las Mañanitas," a beautiful song that celebrates light shining at dawn and birds singing for the person whose birthday it is. That person might be only seven years old, but the song acclaims them as someone whose birth was so important that it caused all the world's flowers to be born! Family members or friends sometimes commission mariachis to gather outside the home of the person having a birthday and serenade them at the break of dawn, calling them to wake up for their special day![7]

At his grandfather's funeral, a younger friend of mine recounted visiting his grandfather's house as a little boy. He would enter the house and his grandfather, with his face lit up and his arms open, would exclaim, "Well, *look* who's here!" It felt to him like his grandfather was celebrating his sheer existence.

115

That's what birthday songs do. By celebrating a person's birth, they celebrate the person's sheer existence.

Christians are especially familiar with birthday singing because of their love for Christmas carols. A carol is a joyful song to celebrate the birth of Jesus, and Christian hymnbooks are rich with them.[8] Some of them have become famous throughout the world and are sung in a great many languages. Christians are not the only people who love and sing them. We can understand why. "O Come, All Ye Faithful" and "Hark! The Herald Angels Sing" are filled with such joy and light that they are irresistible even to people who think Jesus Christ was just a famous man.

The buoyant words of these carols draw people to them. But so does their music. Wonderful composers have brought their best art to Christmas—Bach, Handel, Mendelssohn, and, more recently, Vaughan Williams and Benjamin Britten. The French carol "Angels We Have Heard on High" is sung to music by an unknown eighteenth-century composer and features a glorious refrain ("Gloria in excelsis Deo") with music of cascading joy.

Psalm 98 one more time:

> Shout for joy to the LORD, all the earth,
>   burst into jubilant song with music;
> make music to the LORD with the harp,
>   with the harp and the sound of singing,
> with trumpets and the blast of the ram's horn—
>   shout for joy before the LORD, the King. (vv. 4–6 NIV)

This is what Christians do for the birthday of Jesus. We "burst into jubilant song." We "make music to the Lord" with organs and pianos and trumpets and drums and strings. We sing to-

gether. One of the blessings of Christian worship is that we get to raise our voice in a crowd. So, when a pandemic closes churches, one of the things Christians miss most is congregational singing. Singing at home during remote worship simply doesn't measure up.

Singing with other believers is one of a Christian's primal joys. Is it any wonder that when Johannes Gutenberg invented the printing press in the fifteenth century, one of its early uses was to print hymns so people could read their words and sing their music in harmony? In the Middle Ages, the only singers at Mass were professionals who sang in Latin. But, after Gutenberg's invention, Moravian Christians published a hymnbook in 1501 and Martin Luther published one in 1524 that included four of his own hymns.[9]

We Christians celebrate Christmas with carols. But we also sing our gratitude for Jesus's atoning death with "When I Survey the Wondrous Cross" and for his victorious resurrection with "Christ the Lord Is Risen Today." We sing on Good Friday and Easter. We also sing to celebrate Jesus's ascension and to rejoice on Pentecost. In fact, a major Christian hymnal such as *Lift Up Your Hearts* contains 185 "psalms, hymns, and spiritual songs" to celebrate the major events of Jesus Christ's life, from Advent to Pentecost.[10]

Gifts, Sports, Bands, Parades, and Meals

Grateful people like to celebrate what they are thankful for. They raise their voices to do it. But they also celebrate by other means. They give each other gifts at Christmas, for birthdays, at weddings, and for other special occasions. Of course, gift-giving may become routine. People may give merely because it's expected. But thoughtful gifts are classic expressions of gratitude. By offering a gift, the giver says to the recipient, "I appreciate you. I value you. I want to enhance your life with this token of my enthusiasm for it."

People celebrate with gifts. But also by more raucous means. Watch a college basketball game on TV in which the home team wins—particularly if by an upset—and you will see a familiar form of sports celebration. At the final buzzer, the home team's fans stream out onto the court. They mob their team's players, clapping them on the back. They shout. They applaud. They jump up and down. They hug each other. They raise their arms and wave their banners.

At many of these games, the college pep band plays. In fact, one of the most common reasons for bands to play is in celebration of something people are grateful for. Bands play at sports events, wedding receptions, and anniversary celebrations. They play on village squares to celebrate national holidays. They play "Pomp and Circumstance" at college graduation ceremonies.

They play for other events too. It's hard to imagine a hotel's New Year's Eve celebration without a dance band. International folk festivals (such as Munich's annual Oktoberfest) would be lifeless without their band music. The same goes for Cinco de Mayo, a celebration on May 5 of the Mexican victory over the French in 1862. At least as popular in the United States as in Mexico, the festival abounds in music and dancing. Ostensibly an expression of joy and gratitude for a battle victory, the celebration has evolved into a general celebration of Latin life—much enhanced by lively mariachi bands.

How do grateful people live? They celebrate what they're grateful for. They shout and sing and strike up the band. They also march in parades—one of the showiest forms of human celebration, typically including costumes and floats and motorcycles and open cars with celebrities. Parades have marching bands and street dancing and baton-twirling majorettes and sometimes giant balloon figures that move in the wind above the celebration. If it's a victory parade, there may also be falling ticker tape.

Here are some of the important parades of the world:

- Oktoberfest parades in Germany to celebrate German life
- Cinco de Mayo parades in Mexico, the US, and elsewhere to celebrate Latin life
- Bastille Day military parade in Paris to celebrate the French Revolution
- Fourth of July parades in the US to celebrate American independence
- Independence Day parade in Kyiv, Ukraine, to celebrate Ukrainian independence from the USSR
- Bud Billiken Parade and Picnic in Chicago on the second Saturday of August to celebrate African American life
- Tournament of Roses Parade in Pasadena, California, to celebrate New Year's Day
- Macy's Thanksgiving Day Parade in New York City to celebrate Thanksgiving Day and the traditional start of the Christmas shopping season

Thanksgiving Day parades remind us that this is a feast day in the US. Other countries have harvest feasts too. Japan's

Labor Thanksgiving Day to celebrate the rice harvest started at least two thousand years ago. China's thanksgiving feast goes on for three days. In the US the tradition of annually setting aside a day for thanksgiving is old and deep in the nation's culture, going back to the time of the earliest settlers of Virginia and Massachusetts and anchored to the nation's calendar by proclamations of Presidents Washington and Lincoln.

At the heart of a traditional thanksgiving celebration is a feast. Other celebrations feature food and drink—birthday cake at birthdays, for example, and eggnog at Christmas. Wedding receptions and retirement parties often center on food and drink, as do Christmas and Easter celebrations. In various church traditions Christians observe the "calendar of saints," remembering their heroes of faith by calling those celebration days "feasts," as in "the Feast of St. John the Evangelist." The Jewish Passover seder and the Christian Eucharist celebrate God's mighty acts of deliverance by means of special food and drink.

Why celebrate with food and drink? Why express our gratitude by eating and drinking? Perhaps because food and drink nourish life itself, and grateful people want to be alive and alert to enjoy the gifts they are grateful for. Maybe because food and drink give us joy, and joy is the mood of celebration. Maybe because celebration is a group event, and feasting is a prime method of group bonding.

In any case, meals are a classic way to celebrate, and the Thanksgiving feast is the best-known meal in America. Let's imagine a classic Thanksgiving feast: a family sits around a table on the last Thursday of November, savoring the sight and blended aromas of a twelve-pound, golden-brown roasted turkey with mushroom stuffing, mashed potatoes with pan gravy, buttered corn, fresh bread, garden salad with bacon dressing, pumpkin pie, and other good things. The family is sitting for this meal as an annual habit, but that's nothing against it: it's a sort of glad habit. In many families there are guests—students whose college cafeteria is closed, international guests from church, maybe somebody without a local family. And, blessedly often, each person at the table expresses thanks for something good that came to them during the past year.

Among believers, there's a table prayer of thanksgiving. This may provide unexpected benefits. One of my friends, an award-winning author, remembers a thanksgiving prayer from when he was a boy on Long Island. During the prayer he became aware of faint slurping sounds and opened his eyes to see the family dog with its paws on the table, licking the side of the roasted turkey. My friend then noticed that his grandmother was also watching the spectacle. She looked at her grandson and put her index finger to her lips in the familiar gesture that means "Shhh! Keep quiet about this!" My friend reports that this event became a delightful secret between his grandmother and him—one they shared until her death.

In one of the best passages from Scripture, St. Paul writes to close his letter to the Philippians:

> Finally, beloved, whatever is true, whatever is honorable, whatever is just, whatever is pure, whatever is pleasing, whatever is commendable, if there is any excellence and if there is anything worthy of praise, think about these things. (Phil. 4:8)

"Think about these things"? Of course. Even more, we will savor and celebrate them. Doing so will wonderfully express our gratitude and then increase it.

9

Taking Care

Old Yeller tells the story of a fourteen-year-old boy and his dog. With his father, mother, and five-year-old brother Arliss, Travis Coates lives on a farm in the hill country of Texas in the 1860s amid raccoons, bears, wolves, and feral hogs. When his father leaves for several months on a cattle drive, he tells young Travis that he now has to be "the man of the family," meaning that Travis must look after his younger brother and the work on the farm. Travis's father promises him that if he handles these responsibilities well, he'll be rewarded with his own horse when his father returns, adding that, in the meantime, what Travis needs to help him around the farm is a good dog.

Not long after, a stray dog shows up on the farm, but he doesn't look very good. Skinny and mangy, he has one chewed-off ear and only a short stub of a tail. Travis discovers that this slick-haired, yellow intruder is also a thief. He's climbed a metal barrel and leaped from it to pull down and devour a side of pork the family had hung from the pole rafters of their dog run. And he's unremorseful. When he sees Travis, he runs to him, all wriggly and happy, wagging his tail stub and barking in a way that sounds like human yelling. Because of this and his fur color, Travis calls him "Old Yeller."

Travis doesn't want this friendly thief around but has to admit that Old Yeller's acrobatic method of thievery shows he's a smart dog. He proves to be valuable too. One day, little Arliss is playing in a creek when a bear cub approaches him. Arliss thinks the cub wants to play and grabs his hind leg. The bear cub cries out, which brings his large mama crashing through the brush to save him. Arliss is in peril and Travis, running toward him, can't get there in time to save him. But Old Yeller can. He charges the mama bear, who swats him away with a powerful paw, knocking him head over heels. But Old Yeller keeps charging and at one point hangs by his jaws from the bear's throat just long enough for Travis to swoop in, grab Arliss, and run for home. With the child safe, Old Yeller abandons the fight and runs home too, bounding joyously into the house to lick everybody in the face and yell his head off.

"The way he acted," says Travis, "you might have thought the bear fight hadn't been anything more than a rowdy romp that we'd all taken part in for the fun of it."[1]

Full of gratitude and love for Old Yeller, Travis starts caring for him in wonderful ways. He washes Old Yeller and removes his ticks and fleas. He inspects his dog's paws for thorns and tweezers them out. He welcomes him to sleep in the bed he shares with Arliss. On one occasion, Old Yeller saves Travis from an attack by feral hogs and is himself gravely wounded, his belly ripped open by a hog's canines. Doing what he can, Travis gently eases his dog's entrails back into place and binds him up with strips he rips from his own shirt. He then gradually nurses his beloved companion back toward health.

Alas, in the end Travis has to care for him one last, heart-breaking way. When Old Yeller gets bitten by a rabid wolf, Travis has no choice but to put him down, thus ending one of the most enduring tales of friendship between a boy and his dog in all of children's literature.

Taking Care of What We're Grateful For

Old Yeller shows us that one of the proofs of our gratitude for a beloved animal in our lives is that we take good care of it. What could be more wrong and foolish than neglecting it? What could be more obvious evidence of ingratitude?

Already as children we are taught to take care of our pets, take care of our room, take care of our toys. A parent's voice is always in our head: Don't leave your toys out in the rain. Don't forget to walk the dog. Don't leave stuff all over your room.

From childhood on, in ordinary life with ordinary valuables, we practice the same principles—most of the time. Appreciate having a roof over your head? Don't let wet leaves pile up on it. Grateful for having a car? Change its oil. Appreciate having good friends? See them!

Married couples have abundant reasons to be grateful for their bond. Marriage is a school of virtue. It's a solid structure for raising children. It's a prime form of human community and therefore a strong thread in the fabric of society.

> "Until one has loved an animal a part of one's soul remains unawakened."
>
> —Anatole France[a]

125

What kind of marriage is likeliest to exhibit these virtues?

In a deeply insightful discussion, Robert Roberts presents three models of marriage and heartily recommends one as superior.[2] In the "self-realization model of marriage," each spouse marries for whatever they can get out of the union. Each wants to pull from marriage whatever meets their own needs, and each feels justified in divorcing if their personal growth is in any way stifled.

In the "contract model of marriage," couples make classic vows that elevate their marriage above mere self-realization:

> I promise before God and these witnesses to be your loving and faithful spouse, in plenty and in want, in joy and in sorrow, in sickness and in health, as long as we both shall live.[3]

These promises establish a platform of dependability under the marriage and stabilize life on it. So far so good. But, more recently, couples who make vows along these lines construct them to hedge—sometimes by changing only one word. After all, who can promise to *actually* keep on loving till death? What if she gets MS? What if he goes bankrupt? To hedge, such couples promise to stick it out through thick and thin not "as long as we both shall live" but only "as long as we both shall *love*." The result is something tantamount to "I promise to be your loving spouse until one of us—and it could be me—decides to quit." With this fake promise, the marriage platform is wobbly from the start.

Roberts recommends a specifically Christian alternative— namely, the "one-flesh model of marriage."[4] In it, each spouse deliberately seeks the other's good, knowing that their self-expenditure in the interests of the other is actually a recipe

"Married couples can help each other cook, clean, and shop. But they should not attempt to hang wallpaper together."

—Anonymous[b]

for their own thriving too. We find ourselves by spending ourselves. We can let ourselves go for the sake of the other in the confidence that, if we do, we'll get ourselves back.

In a telling example, Roberts suggests that well-married couples don't merely tolerate each other's particular interests. They try to share them.[5] Let's say she loves art and he loves baseball. He accompanies her on gallery tours and asks her to share what she finds striking in them. She goes to games with him and asks him to explain what's going on in them. Each spouse treasures the interest of the other and both find that practicing marriage this way strengthens it.

Grateful couples take care of their marriage. They look at each other and speak to each other with unmistakable respect. They don't imagine slights. When a decision is to be made, they confer at whatever length is necessary and often defer to the spouse more naturally competent on the issue to be decided. They are quick to praise and slow to criticize. They keep each other's secrets. They protect each other's reputation. They practice sexual and emotional faithfulness. They rejoice and weep together.

Taking Care of Our Faith

Marriage is a prime example of this chapter's principle—that we show our gratitude for good things by taking care of them.

The more valuable the goods, the better the care. So it is with our Christian faith. The work of the Holy Spirit ties us to Jesus Christ from God's side of the bond. From our side, it's faith. Like so much of value in the Christian life, faith is both God's gift and our calling. There's no doubt it's a gift. Jesus taught that "no one can come to me unless drawn by the Father who sent me" (John 6:44). But faith is also our calling. Jesus says so with a simple imperative: "Believe in God, believe also in me" (John 14:1).

Every Christian comes to know that this imperative is bigger than we are. We know the drag of doubt and sloth. We know what it's like to be spiritually depressed—to find the universe emptied of God and our lives emptied of joy. We know how the presence of advanced evil in the world can taint our trust in God's providence.

So we pray for God to rejuvenate us. We practice spiritual disciplines that centuries of Christian saints have told us will help. We pray when we don't feel like it. We go on spiritual retreat because we know we should. We meditate on God's Word, hoping for a ray of light. We take long, slow walks through cemeteries, treading six feet above well-dressed skeletons while soberly reflecting on how—if there is no God and no eternal life—human life simply stops.

All these means are part of traditional spiritual hygiene, and they are all an immeasurable help when it comes to taking good care of our faith.

According to the letters of St. Paul, the centerpiece of such caretaking is mortifying our old nature and vivifying our new one. This is the recipe for Christian sanctification as we saw in chapter 5 in connection with dying and rising with Christ. We died and rose with Christ when he did because he is the "second Adam," our representative. We did it again in our baptism, a ceremony that sacramentally binds us to the dying and rising Christ. And we do it every day when we put our sins to death—kill them, mortify them, crucify them—and bring our virtues to life—encourage them, vivify them, "clothe ourselves" with them (Col. 3:5, 12).

Sanctification is God's work in us. But it's also our work in us. Scripture says both things. Jesus "cleanses us from all sin" but only if we "walk in the light" (1 John 1:7).

There's no better way to walk in the light than by putting our sins to death. All serious Christians have experience trying to do it. Suppose my besetting sin is conceit. I am too wily to say it out loud, but I secretly think I'm hot stuff. I think I'm better than others—and if others don't know it, they should. I might motor along with this superior attitude for years until something jolts me awake.

If it does, I know I have to kill my conceit. I have to yoke my efforts to the purifying work of the Holy Spirit in me. So I meditate on the superlative greatness of God and look at myself by contrast. I meditate on the superlative *grace* of God and see that I have nothing good that wasn't given to me. I confess my conceit to God and lament it and beg to be rid of it. I start deliberately praising others, recognizing their gifts and good character. I spend time outdoors where nonhuman creation seems to hum along just fine without paying any attention to me. And I begin to see my conceit as laughable.

How does mortifying my conceit show and strengthen my faith? When I put my conceit to death, I trust God's Word that doing so is not only right but also healthy. Mortifying oneself is no fun at all. It's mortifying. But I do it anyway because I

"I am not conceited. Conceit is a fault and I have no faults."

—David Lee Roth[c]

trust God that doing it is life-giving, that it will actually make life *better*.

And it does. As I kill off my conceit, I find that God seems closer to me. Other people seem more interesting to me. Squirrels leaping from branches seem more delightful to me. I've broken out of the tiny cabin of my own self-involvement and have found the whole universe come alive as I turn to it.

When I reflect on this wonderful exercise of dying and rising, I become more grateful for my faith that motivated me to tackle it in the first place. And I want to keep looking for ways to take good care of it.

"Delight to Do Every Kind of Good"

Gratitude is the Christian's natural response to God. God has created and redeemed us and is now sanctifying us through the work of the Holy Spirit. In response, we are grateful. We are grateful for an abundance of gifts—for family members and work and good friends and the beauty of nature to humble and inspire us. Even when life is troubled, there is almost always something inside the trouble we can be grateful for.

One natural impulse of grateful people is generosity. Having received so much that's good, we want to do good to others. The Heidelberg Catechism—a confessional jewel of the Protestant Reformation—states that "we do good . . . so that in all our living we may show that we are thankful to God for all he has done for us." In fact, we *"delight* to do every kind of good as God wants us to."[6]

"Do-gooding" has gotten bad press in some circles because some attempts to do good can be intrusive or even counterproductive—maybe "fixing what ain't broke" or "bringing a fire hose to a flood." Some do-gooders are busybodies whose attempts to help feel a lot like interference. They want to help in the worst way.

But the call to do good for others—real, actual good—is central to the Christian religion. Some of us will recall one of Jesus's most famous imperatives: "Let your light shine before others, so that they may see your good works and give glory to your Father in heaven" (Matt. 5:16). Centuries of Christians have called attention to Jesus's teaching on this subject.

In 1746 Jonathan Edwards, America's greatest theologian, wrote a book in order to judge a dispute.[7] The dispute centered on how to think of the Great Awakening, a huge New England revival of the 1730s and '40s in which Edwards himself had taken a leading role. When the Great Awakening spread through New England in 1740, a number of strange new happenings began to occur. People started to sob and faint at religious meetings. They trembled and groaned. Some got "high on the Spirit" and began to twist and shout. Enthusiastic believers within the Great Awakening of the 1740s were *sure* their faith was attaching to Christ. Couldn't they feel it? Couldn't they feel their own joy and certainty?

Edwards found himself at the center of a dispute. On the one hand, some people looked at the controversial signs and saw religious nonsense. Some saw madness or fraud or even demonic possession. Many ordinary Reformed people questioned the new ways of carrying on. Did the commotion fit with what Paul calls "a sober and right mind" (1 Cor. 15:34)? Was it even decent?

On the other hand, some people looked at the controversial signs and saw the power of the Holy Spirit at work. If a dignified member of the community started rolling in the aisle of the church, wouldn't it have to be the Holy Spirit that got him rolling? Edwards himself knew from experience that if a person is born again, this supernatural event will show itself in a whole new life. Some of Edwards's supporters believed that such conversion would come with the force of Pentecost. New and strange signs of revival were to be expected, even welcomed.

Edwards's task was to judge the dispute between people who said the controversial accompaniments of the Great Awakening were signs of the presence of God and other people who said these things were signs of the presence of hysteria, or worse.

After a lengthy search of Scripture, Edwards reached his conclusion and wrote it up in *The Religious Affections*. In his book, Edwards concluded that the controversial signs tell us little. Given our tendency toward self-deception, we can't tell whether the signs come from God or from our own overheated imaginations or from somewhere else. If we want to test for true religion, shaking and rolling are neither here nor there. Take them or leave them, said Edwards, but don't hang anything of significance on them, because the Bible's interest lies somewhere else.

The Christian's Central Business

So where *does* the Bible's interest lie? How may we judge our own godliness and its sincerity? How may we judge our own *gratitude* and its sincerity? According to Edwards, the way to tell whether we have been truly born again by the Spirit of God is to see whether we have a godly practice. Do we have in our lives a pattern of good works governed by the Ten Commandments and other biblical guides? Do we make good deeds our "central business" the way physicians make medicine their central business? Do we keep on in our practice of godliness for the long run of our lives, and not just in little spurts while other people are watching?[8]

To follow Jesus we have to practice what he preached. What Jesus preached is that a good tree is known by its fruit—not by its twigs or leaves or heaving branches. Christians are known by their godly practice, not by their good intentions or pious talk or spiritual hand-waving. A good tree is known by producing actual fruit, and a good Christian is known by producing actual good works. "Godliness consists not in a heart which intends to do the will of God but in a heart which *does* it."[9]

But can't good works have shabby motives? Can't people make a show of them, try to get credit for them, and go after them not to *do* good but just to *look* good?

Absolutely. To see whether we have the Spirit of Christ in us and not just the spirit of self-advertising, we should ask whether our good deeds cost us something. Are we willing to accept the pain of new life as well as its joy?

- Do we give money away that we would rather have kept, and do we (eventually) find satisfaction in doing so?
- Do we accept other people's suffering as a shared burden and help them with it?

- Do we thirst for justice in the world and inconvenience ourselves to seek and support it?
- Do we praise freely and complain rarely?
- Do we put the best face on other people's motives while also suspecting our own?

Only God knows a human heart. But we can see a Christian practice. Generally speaking, we can tell a good heart by good deeds that express the fruit of the Spirit: love, joy, peace, patience, kindness, generosity, faithfulness, gentleness, and self-control.

By thinking as he did, Edwards joined a long line of people who speak the Christian faith with a Reformed accent. Reformed Christians put a lot of emphasis on disciplined holiness as the center of a Christian life—not how you talk but how you walk; not how you feel but how you act. John Calvin taught that the main function of the Ten Commandments is not to make us feel guilty but to guide us in a straight Christian walk.[10] Before worship styles changed, many Reformed churches included a reading of the Ten Commandments for just this reason. The law of God is a grace of God, mercifully pointing out the things (stealing, lying, idolizing) that grieve God and wreck life, and others (worshiping God, keeping Sabbath, protecting our neighbor's reputation) that please God and build life.

Glad Counsels for New People

I think we all understand that the practice of disciplined holiness grows out of faith. It takes *faith* to believe that we have been born again by the Spirit of God. It takes *faith* to believe that our old nature is doomed and that one day our bad old habits will fall away. Perhaps above all, it takes *faith* to believe that God loved us deeply "while we still were sinners" (Rom. 5:8).[11]

Full of such faith, a Christian overflows with gratitude and, from it, tries to please God, to glorify God, to attract others to God by doing all kinds of good. It remains true all along that we are justified by grace alone and through faith alone. Good works don't save anybody. But they are much more than a pleasant option. Doing good works is, in fact, our central business.

I know that such talk makes some of us nervous. (It makes Lutheran brothers and sisters *extremely* nervous.) What if focusing attention on good works should lead us away from faith in Jesus Christ and into an obsession with our own spiritual hygiene? What if we lose interest in the goodness of God and get fascinated by merit badges instead? What if we end up trying to graft a Ben Franklin program of self-improvement onto a confession of the grace of Jesus Christ?

We are right to worry about do-it-yourself religion, and some of today's Christian book and sermon titles (variants of "How to Make Your Life a Big, Fat Success") feed our concern. Yet, despite dangers and abuses, an emphasis on sanctification is still entirely right. We can see this if we just open our Bibles and read the New Testament. What we find there is a host of glad counsels for those who would follow Jesus:

- "Let your light shine before others, so that they may see your good works." (Matt. 5:16)
- "Hate what is evil, hold fast to what is good." (Rom. 12:9)

- "Whatever is true, whatever is honorable . . . think about these things." (Phil. 4:8)
- "Pursue righteousness." (2 Tim. 2:22)
- "Clothe yourselves with compassion." (Col. 3:12)
- "Forgive each other." (Col. 3:13)
- "Strive first for the kingdom of God." (Matt. 6:33)
- "Bear one another's burdens, and in this way you will fulfill the law of Christ." (Gal. 6:2)

How striking that the gospel of grace is full of practical commandments to do good! In a secular frame of mind, we chafe under God's commandments. They nick our pride and cramp our style. We think they're for children. In a secular frame of mind, we think of obedience as distasteful—a cowardly knuckling under to somebody else's will.

But, paradoxical as it sounds, the truth is that God's counsels bring us God's grace because they make us free. Sin traps us. Godly obedience liberates us. God's counsels are guides to a free and flourishing life. They say, "Do this and you will thrive." Or they say, "Don't do this: it'll kill you."

How do I take care of my faith? One of the best ways is to mortify sinful habits and to vivify righteous ones such as doing good deeds. If I do good deeds regularly, they become a practice. Over time my practice becomes a habit. If I make a habit of doing good works—especially the ones I don't really want to do—I strengthen my character and my faith along with it.

How so? Doing good works strengthens my faith that Jesus Christ's program for my life will actually make it better. Doing good works is part of rising with Christ, and if I rise with Christ in this way, I discover that my world brightens. I sense that I'm a productive citizen of God's kingdom. I see that I am helping others to thrive, and the sight gives me joy. I *trust* God's teaching that I will flourish only by causing others to flourish.

Good works are the best evidence of our gratitude to God, wrote Jonathan Edwards. They are the central business of a Christian's life. He might have added that this is the one business that will outlast every recession.

10

A Cornucopia of Gifts

At traditional Thanksgiving Day feasts, the table's centerpiece is sometimes a cornucopia: a hollow, horn-shaped wicker basket spilling over with the fruit of the autumn harvest. The word "cornucopia" comes from Latin and means "a horn of plenty." A typical cornucopia might include grapes, apples, nuts, mini pumpkins, gourds, wheat stalks, ears of sweet corn, and sunflowers. It's a splendid symbol of harvested abundance and therefore a compelling picture of how many good things there are to be thankful for.

In this final chapter I want to offer a sampling of these things.

They Had Never Given Up

In the summer of 2022 my colleague Kathleen Smith received a phone call from an officer in the United States Army. An identity specialist from the Casualty and Mortuary Affairs Division told Kathleen that, after DNA testing, the army had made a positive identification of the remains of her uncle, US Army Pfc. Donald Hofman, age nineteen, of Grand Rapids, Michigan, who had been killed during the last months of World War II.

According to the army's press release,[1] in January 1945, Hofman's infantry division joined five companies trying to hold terrain near Reipertswiller, France, when they were surrounded by German forces that attacked them with artillery fire. Their commander ordered the surrounded companies to try a breakout, but only two men escaped through German lines. The rest were either captured or killed. Hofman was among those killed, but his body could not be recovered because of the German occupation of the area.

Beginning in 1946, the American Graves Registration Command, the organization that hunted for and recovered fallen American personnel in the European Theater, searched the area near Reipertswiller and found thirty-seven unidentified sets of American remains. But it was unable to identify any of them as Hofman and declared him unrecoverable on May 22, 1951.

Army historians have since been conducting ongoing research into soldiers missing from combat around Reipertswiller and found that Unknown X-6376, buried at Ardennes American Cemetery in Belgium, could be Hofman. X-6376 was disinterred in July 2021 and transferred to the laboratory at Offutt Air Force Base, Nebraska, for analysis. On July 8, 2022, the lab positively identified the remains. Unknown X-6376 was US Army Pfc. Donald Hofman.

Hofman's name is recorded on the Walls of the Missing at Epinal American Cemetery, an American Battle Monuments Commission site in Dinozé, France, along with others still missing from World War II. The army has promised that a rosette will be placed next to his name to indicate he has been accounted for.

On October 8, 2022, Hofman's family laid his body to rest in the Winchester Cemetery in Byron Township, Michigan. Included in the gathering was Rev. Leonard Hofman, Donald's sole surviving brother, who had given a DNA sample in 2013 that enabled the identification of his brother's remains and who spoke movingly of growing up with his brother. He remarked that during his life Donald had never been given much tribute—not till now, not till he was being buried a war hero for giving his life for his country.

The army was at the cemetery to honor Pfc. Hofman by firing a gun salute, displaying the colors, and playing taps. In the presence of autumn colors and a stiff breeze, the gathering of family and friends heard Psalm 90, sang "Great Is Thy Faithfulness," and listened as Rev. Kathleen Smith brought a message of gratitude and hope. In her message, Kathleen spoke of her uncle's profession of faith in church during his last home service and of the Christian's sure and certain hope of the resurrection of the dead.

Kathleen expressed her family's immense gratitude to the United States Army. For all the many decades after World War II, the army never forgot Pfc. Donald Hofman. They gathered his remains and waited, almost as if they anticipated that one day new technology might identify him. When DNA technology was developed, the army made the positive identification, notified Donald's family, and buried their soldier with full military honors.

As I stood in the cemetery that October day, I marveled at what I was seeing. Seventy-seven years after Donald Hofman's

"To this day, more than 73,000 troops remain missing from World War II alone. . . . Most of them will never be found. But the search, though it may be in vain, will never end. The oath to never leave a fallen comrade is a promise made to each other, that even if we die, our brothers in arms will do everything they can to bring us home. It's a mission that hasn't ended, and as long as wars continue, it never will."

—Nate Rawlings[a]

death, the US Army was honoring one of their own at his proper burial. They had not left their soldier behind. They had not forgotten him. They had never given up.

The Largest Lake in the United States

All of us are inclined to take for granted the valuable things closest to us. We don't *always* take these treasures for granted, but we tend to. Kids who grow up in the Swiss Alps may think of mountain skiing as routine, while kids on the Gold Coast of Australia think the same of ocean surfing. Maybe youngsters in New York City think everybody has a Yankee Stadium and a Radio City Music Hall. The same goes for those living close to any number of treasures, such as woods and streams and prairie flowers.

I grew up in Grand Rapids, Michigan. What contributes to the city's appeal is that it's only a short distance from the eastern shore of Lake Michigan, the largest lake inside the United States and the largest lake inside the borders of any country in the world. You can't see across it—a fact that impresses first-time visitors unaccustomed to wide inland lakes. It delights sport fishers with its abundance of steelhead and brown trout, coho and Chinook salmon. It supplies drinking water for millions, including the city of Chicago. When I was a boy in Grand Rapids and would leave a faucet on or a hose running, my dad would say something like, "Son, don't waste our good Lake Michigan water." He was aware of it and thankful for it. I needed to learn that from him and later teach it to my own sons.

The eastern shore of the lake is famous for its sandy beaches and dunes. In fact, its three hundred miles of sandy dunes are unique in the world. The shore is also dotted with picturesque lighthouses and bordered by leafy state parks and bustling beach towns. Moreover, the southern and northern ends of the lake moderate their regions' temperatures to a degree suitable for grapes and wineries. All along the length of the lake, beach town marinas provide dockage for vessels of all kinds, including an array of graceful sailboats.

Near the northern end of the lake, Sleeping Bear Dunes National Lakeshore features towering dunes and winding trails, lush forests for hiking and clear streams for kayaking. The area is known for biking and birding and dune climbing. In the winter, people ski, snowshoe, and slide their toboggans down the dunes.

Summer weather draws visitors to the eastern shore of Lake Michigan from all over the world. It draws summer residents even from Chicago and Milwaukee—cities on the opposite side of the lake. The reason for their trek around the bottom of the lake is that prevailing west winds blow the warmer surface water of Lake Michigan to its eastern shore, making for wonderful summer swimming.

On a hot July day at the lake, my brother and my friends and I would run and jump in the shallow water, turn somersaults

"The Great Lakes—Superior, Huron, Michigan, Ontario and Erie—make up the largest body of fresh water on Earth, accounting for one-fifth of the freshwater surface on the planet at 6 quadrillion gallons. The area of all the Great Lakes is 95,160 square miles and spans 750 miles from west to east. The square mileage is larger than the state of Texas. . . . About 14,000 years ago, the Great Lakes area was covered with a glacier that was more than a half-mile thick. As the glacier melted, it slowly moved toward Canada and left behind a series of large depressions that filled with water. These formed the basic shape of the Great Lakes, and about 10,000 years ago the Great Lakes took the form that is familiar today."

—Kim Ann Zimmerman[b]

in the deeper water, splash each other, lie in the warm sand, build sandcastles, wreck each other's sandcastles, race along the shore, and throw beach balls. I was blissfully unaware of Lake Michigan's unique status and international appeal. All I knew was that it provided the kind of joy without which summer was not complete.

Five Little Things

The US Army's persistence in leaving no soldier behind and the largest lake in the United States are good-sized blessings to be received with equal-sized gratitude. But most blessings are smaller and most are available to all of us—not just to army soldiers' families or to people with access to Lake Michigan. Here are five I like:

- YouTube videos of dogs howling to accompany their owner's music.

- Pink rhododendron blossoms of a size somewhere between a softball and a volleyball.
- Friends who would never say, "I told you so."
- The fact that people have multiple kinds of intelligence beyond verbal and mathematical, including social intelligence, mechanical intelligence, and musical intelligence.[2]
- A seven-year-old boy saying grace before dinner as follows: "Dear Lord, thank you for Halloween. Please be with the people who have never heard of it."

Doctors Without Borders

One of the ways we show gratitude for great humanitarian organizations is by contributing money to them. The money expresses our enthusiasm for what these organizations themselves contribute to the world. Among the highest ranked of such charities is Doctors Without Borders (DWB), a medical assistance program without peer.

Established in Geneva in 1971, DWB sends physicians, nurses, and logistics experts across the globe to wherever they are needed.[3] Their small salaries make them almost volunteers. These medical experts offer treatment to people without access to care, to people suffering from violent conflicts, epidemics, and natural disasters.

In war zones, DWB personnel don't take sides. They just meet needs. In natural disaster zones such as those created by floods, earthquakes, and hurricanes, victims almost immediately lose access to health care. DWB teams provide a rapid response. During epidemics such as COVID, DWB's medical staff brings treatment and vaccines while the logistics experts provide sanitation services.

Some of the people that DWB staff serves are refugees fleeing war or persecution. On the edge of perishing, they desperately need lifesaving care. DWB teams are there for them.

They also help with maternal medical care in developing nations. In many of them, childbirth is far from routine. So DWB teams offer prenatal consultations, emergency obstetrics care, and postnatal follow-up, especially for the perils of infection and hemorrhage.

Because much of the world is ill-fed, DWB teams track hunger zones across the globe and set up an outpost to screen for malnutrition, establish outpatient clinics, and serve patients with ready-to-use kits of therapeutic food.

One of the main problems facing medical caregivers these days is that many bacterial infections no longer respond to standard antibiotic treatment. In some places antibiotics are overused, are used for too short a time, or have substandard strength in over-the-counter versions. In these settings, DWB personnel labor to curb bacterial infections with vaccines and by providing safer water and better sanitation. They also educate the populace about responsible and effective use of antibiotics.

DWB teams have to be versatile and knowledgeable about a range of maladies across the world. They treat Ebola and HIV/AIDS; cholera, measles, meningitis, and monkeypox; kala-azar and malaria—the deadliest parasitic disease in the world.

Doctors Without Borders are brave people. They go to some of the toughest places on earth, risk exposure to conflict and deadly disease, and bring their expertise to people they do not know. Their generosity makes news in heaven. It causes thanksgiving everywhere they go.

Five Things Good Cops Do

Who besides DWB teams have a vocation to be brave? Firefighters. Soldiers like Donald Hofman. Those who protest against dictators. People with hard lives who soldier on without complaint. Believers facing persecution.

And, of course, cops. They're often in the news, sometimes for acting badly. Very badly. Kneeling on the neck of a suspect until he's dead. Bullying or beating or shooting innocent citizens. Mistreating minorities in racist ways. These are abhorrent offenses made worse by the fact that they are perpetrated by officers of the law.

At the same time, good cops have to take a lot of abuse from people who resent that there is anybody at all who enforces the law. Parts of major cities are full of violent anti-cop graffiti. These are the same parts of the cities in which cops regularly risk their lives to protect innocent citizens. Every day, good cops have to live with the fact that the rogue minority on the force taints the reputation of the honorable majority.

From everything I can find on the subject, I've come to believe that most cops in the US are honest and fair. They really do protect and serve the public. Many go out of their way to show compassion to people who need it. Here are five examples of good things cops do. I've drawn them from a conversation with a much-decorated sergeant on the police force of a major American city:

- Good cops stay with gunshot victims and comfort them. These cops say to the victim something like,

"I'm with you now and I won't leave you. I think you're going to be all right."

- Good cops won't talk down to suspects and especially not in front of the suspect's spouse and kids. They show respect.
- Good cops go through the rooms of an elderly person who has died and remove anything (illegal drugs, pornography) that the deceased would have been ashamed for their children and grandchildren to find. A good cop bags it and discards it in their station's dumpster.
- Good cops use the minimum necessary force to capture a suspect, sometimes at peril to themselves.
- Good cops stay calm in a highly charged situation, refusing to react to the provocations of a suspect and taking calculated steps to de-escalate tension.

I'm indignant about bad cops but grateful for good ones. I'm grateful that good ones outnumber bad ones perhaps nine to one. I'm grateful for their compassion. And I'm grateful when they are brave.

Called to Be Prime Citizens of the Kingdom

Any cornucopia of blessings would include thousands that no book has space to publish. I've chosen to write about Pfc. Donald Hofman, Lake Michigan, Doctors Without Borders, and good cops as examples. You would have a different array of samples. So would anybody else. This just goes to show that God and God's human intermediaries have blessed us with enough good things to trigger our gratitude for as long as we live.

For my last example, I want to talk about something I believe is close to the heart of every thoughtful teen and adult—namely, how to live with purpose in the world, how to find meaning in it, how to get up in the morning looking forward to doing something constructive.

All kinds of people have all kinds of purposes for their lives, conscious or not. Getting high. Making lots of money. Being happy. Getting noticed. Being envied. Being respected. Finding fulfilling work. Cultivating a network of friends. Raising a flourishing family. Living so as to "glorify God and enjoy him forever."[4]

These purposes exist on a spectrum from least to most worthy. But those whose purposes rank past the middle of the spectrum would probably agree that *having* a life's purpose makes them grateful. Maybe some of them would thank fate or their lucky stars. Or maybe their parents. Some would thank God. Regardless, these people's natural response to having a purpose in life is thankfulness.

We Christians are no different. We have a purpose Jesus gave us: "Strive first for the kingdom of God" (Matt. 6:33). Following Jesus in this commission gives us our purpose and therefore a huge reason for gratitude. What's more, many other purposes fit inside this uber-purpose. Finding fulfilling work, raising a thriving family, cultivating a network of friends, and living so as to "glorify God and enjoy him forever" are all *examples* of striving first for the kingdom of God.

Let's call Christians who accept Jesus's commission *good citizens* of the kingdom. Everybody is a citizen of the kingdom, whether they know it or not, just because the earth is the Lord's and God rules over all. But Christians who accept Jesus's commission and seriously attempt to follow it are good citizens, prime citizens, model citizens. They have a calling in life and they pursue it with energy.

These are people who have been penetrated by the Spirit of God so that they are redeemed all the way downtown in their hearts. They love God. They love their neighbors. Even when they don't like their neighbors, they love them by treating them well. They hunger for justice. They read Scripture with an appetite and ponder it with respect. They hate cruelty and join efforts to oppose it. They love kindness and support groups that show it. They know that God's kingdom project is to make things right in the world, and they want to be part of that project.

How might they be part of it?

- By going after the knowledge, skills, and attitudes they need to join God's project of making things right.
- By volunteering to help build houses for people who can't otherwise afford them.
- By worshiping God with concentration and love.
- By caring for God's good creation and joining others who do the same.
- By taking an interest in word-and-deed evangelism across the world and supporting it.
- By voting for political candidates who show integrity when it comes to justice for minorities.
- By leaving positive and calming comments on social media.
- By choosing an occupation that is fulfilling in part because it meshes well with God's project in the world.

- By raising a family with tender care and spending themselves to help friends flourish.
- By volunteering for a suicide prevention line.
- By glorifying God—that is, by letting their good deeds enhance God's reputation in the world.

Christians who do things like these have a calling. They have a *purpose* and they get after it. Reading and hearing Scripture in faith, they believe that what lies ahead of us at the end is the full coming of the kingdom of God. The Hebrew Bible testifies that one day God will fill the earth with justice, harmony, and delight (Isa. 2:4; 11:6, 9; 32:15; 65:19–22). This is the blessed state of *shalom*, of universal flourishing, wholeness, and joy—all according to God's purpose and all under the arch of God's blessing and love. *Shalom* is the Hebrew way of spelling the full coming of the kingdom of God. Christians believe that God will one day make it happen, so they gather themselves and go to work in the same direction as they believe.

"Strive first for the kingdom of God." If we Christians accept Jesus's commission, we will never run out of good things to do.

Fulfilling our purpose in life, we will feel needed.

Feeling needed, we will feel valuable.

Feeling valuable, we will feel grateful.

All along, we are buoyed by the knowledge that the good things we do for others make *them* grateful too, in round after round of joy.

151

Jesus said many famous things. Thousands of books have been written about them. Millions of sermons have centered on them. Hundreds of millions of Christians have followed them. But for a Christian's life purpose, one saying leads the way: "Strive first for the kingdom of God."

Could there be a better assignment?

Acknowledgments

Thank you to Rebecca DeYoung, Lee Hardy, Scott Hoezee, John Ortberg, Amy Plantinga Pauw, Robert C. Roberts, Jack Roeda, and James Vanden Bosch, whose comments have enlightened me. Thank you to David Bratt and Laura Bardolph Hubers of BBH Literary, who expertly managed this project from the outset. Thank you to oversight colleagues at the Calvin Institute of Christian Worship—John Witvliet, Kathleen Smith, Kristen Verhulst, and Maria Cornou—who encouraged me to write on gratitude. Thank you to Charlotte vanOyen-Witvliet, who guided me into the rich world of positive psychology. Above all, thank you to Kathleen Plantinga, my wife, who read chapters as they were written and proposed edits that have greatly strengthened the manuscript.

Notes

Chapter 1 What Is Gratitude?

1. Scott Pelley, "Hope Chicago: Charity Sending Students from Chicago High Schools to College for Free," *60 Minutes*, CBS News, August 14, 2022, https://www.cbsnews.com/news/hope-chicago-free-college-students-parents-60-minutes-2022-08-14.

2. Charlotte vanOyen-Witvliet, speaking at a seminar titled "Gratitude: Thankfulness as a Theme in Christian Preaching and Worship" (Calvin University, Grand Rapids, MI, July 24–28, 2017), citing M. E. McCullough, R. A. Emmons, and J. A. Tsang, "The Grateful Disposition: A Conceptual and Empirical Topography," *Journal of Personality and Social Psychology* 82, no. 1 (2002): 112–27. VanOyen-Witvliet noted that for believers, gratitude density includes God, the ultimate giver.

3. Robert C. Roberts, *Spiritual Emotions: A Psychology of Christian Virtues* (Grand Rapids: Eerdmans, 2007), 131.

4. Conversation with philosopher Rebecca Konyndyk DeYoung, July 28, 2020; conversation with philosopher Lee Hardy, February 9, 2021; Robert C. Roberts, "The Blessings of Gratitude," in *The Psychology of Gratitude*, ed. Robert A. Emmons and Michael E. McCullough (Oxford: Oxford University Press, 2004), 63.

5. Solomon Schimmel, "Gratitude in Judaism," in Emmons and McCullough, *Psychology of Gratitude*, 31.

6. Margaret Visser, *The Gift of Thanks: The Roots and Rituals of Gratitude* (Boston: Houghton Mifflin Harcourt, 2009), 85. Faked surprise is not always deceptive; it can be merely playful.

7. John Calvin, *Institutes of the Christian Religion* 3.10.2, ed. John T. McNeill, trans. Ford Lewis Battles, 2 vols. (Philadelphia: Westminster, 1960), 1:720–21.

8. In a conversation on October 10, 2022, my friend James Vanden Bosch, a language expert, observed that "much obliged" was a common response to a favor in nineteenth-century America and can still be heard today in films, especially Westerns, set in that century.

9. Terrance McConnell, *Gratitude* (Philadelphia: Temple University Press, 1993), 50.

Chapter 2 How Do We Get Gratitude?

1. Danielle Slutsky and Misha Slutsky, "Dayenu with English, Hebrew, and Transliteration," Haggadot.com, https://www.haggadot.com/clip/dayenu-english-hebrew-and-transliteration.

2. Solomon Schimmel, "Gratitude in Judaism," in *The Psychology of Gratitude*, ed. Robert A. Emmons and Michael E. McCullough (Oxford: Oxford University Press, 2004), 40.

3. This widely quoted wisdom saying has been attributed to Aesop and to Melody Beattie, and it is often repeated without attribution. I found it in Robert A. Emmons and Joanna Hill, *Words of Gratitude for Mind, Body, and Soul* (Conshohocken, PA: Templeton, 2001), 20, where it is attributed to Beattie.

4. John 1:1, 18; 1 Cor. 16:22; Col. 1:15; 2:9; Heb. 1:3, 6.

5. Robert C. Roberts, *Spiritual Emotions: A Psychology of Christian Virtues* (Grand Rapids: Eerdmans, 2007), 133.

6. Wikipedia, s.v. "I Walk the Line," last modified April 11, 2023, https://en.wikipedia.org/wiki/I_Walk_the_Line.

7. Ken Bazyn, *The Seven Perennial Sins and Their Offspring* (London: Continuum, 2002), 22–23.

8. David G. Allan, "How to Become More Grateful, and Why That Will Make You Happier, Healthier, and More Resilient," CNN, May 19, 2022, https://www.cnn.com/2022/05/19/health/gratitude-wisdom-project-chasing-life-wellness/index.html.

9. Robert A. Emmons, *Thanks! How Practicing Gratitude Can Make You Happier* (Boston: Houghton Mifflin, 2008), 189–90. The title of Emmons's book is misleading and possibly chosen by its publisher to sell books. It is not a happiness how-to book but a thoughtful exploration of a multifaceted virtue.

10. Allan, "How to Become More Grateful."

11. Terrance McConnell, *Gratitude* (Philadelphia: Temple University Press, 1993), 86.

12. C. S. Lewis, *Mere Christianity* (New York: Macmillan, 1960), 161, cited in Gilbert C. Meilaender, *The Theory and Practice of Virtue* (Notre Dame, IN: University of Notre Dame Press, 1984), 15.

Chapter 3 What Blocks My Gratitude?

1. Long thought to have been authored by American theologian Reinhold Niebuhr, the prayer's origin has lately been disputed. An account of the dispute appears in Laurie Goodstein, "Serenity Prayer Stirs Up Doubt: Who Wrote It?," *New York Times*, July 11, 2008, https://www.nytimes.com/2008/07/11/us/11prayer.html.

2. *Alcoholics Anonymous* (New York: Alcoholics Anonymous World Services, 2001), available at https://www.aa.org/the-big-book.

3. Robert A. Caro, *The Path to Power*, vol. 1 of *The Years of Lyndon Johnson* (New York: Vintage, 1990), xviii, xx, 95–96, 110–12. Caro's volumes on Johnson are supreme examples of the biographer's art.

4. Dorothy L. Sayers, "The Other Six Deadly Sins," in *Letters to a Diminished Church* (Nashville: Thomas Nelson, 2004), 103.

5. In a much-discussed article, Peter Wehner describes how political resentments have in recent years been dividing—or even tearing apart—evangelical churches. Peter Wehner, "The Evangelical Church Has Been Breaking Apart," *The Atlantic*, October 24, 2021, https://www.theatlantic.com/ideas/archive/2021/10/evangelical-trump-christians-politics/620469.

6. Silver-medal syndrome includes hanging my head, looking sour, and refusing to congratulate the gold-medal winner.

7. *Amadeus*, screenplay by Peter Shaffer, directed by Milos Forman, Orion Pictures, 1984.

8. Ajani Bazile, "Twenty People Who Are So Entitled They've Already Made 2022 Hell for Others," *BuzzFeed*, July 20, 2022, https://www.buzzfeed.com/ajanibazile/entitled-people-2022.

9. "'She Dropped Her Child Off with Scarlet Fever': 28 Teachers Who Have Dealt with the Worst, Most Entitled Parents," Yahoo! News, November 5, 2022, https://news.yahoo.com/she-dropped-her-child-off-001602243.html.

10. "'She Dropped Her Child Off.'"

11. Michael J. Sandel, *The Tyranny of Merit: What's Become of the Common Good?* (New York: Farrar, Straus & Giroux, 2020), 5.

12. Sandel, *Tyranny of Merit*, 176–82.

Chapter 4 What Happens to Me If I Am Grateful?

1. John Claypool, "Life Is a Gift," in *A Chorus of Witnesses: Model Sermons for Today's Preacher*, ed. Thomas G. Long and Cornelius Plantinga Jr. (Grand Rapids: Eerdmans, 1994), 126.

2. Claypool, "Life Is a Gift," 124.

3. Claypool, "Life Is a Gift," 129.

4. J. R. R. Tolkien, *The Lord of the Rings*, part 3, *The Return of the King* (New York: Ballantine, 1965), 171.

5. "Humility" comes from the Latin word *humus*, which means "earth."

6. Isaac Watts, "Joy to the World," in *Lift Up Your Hearts: Psalms, Hymns, and Spiritual Songs* (Grand Rapids: Faith Alive, 2013), #92. Jonathan Edwards wrote that we *sing* what's in our hearts instead of just saying it not only to express our joy but also to excite it. Jonathan Edwards, *The Religious Affections* (Edinburgh: Banner of Truth, 1986), 44.

7. Christopher Wordsworth, "Alleluia! Alleluia! Hearts to Heaven," in *Lift Up Your Hearts*, #179.

8. John of Damascus, trans. John Mason Neale, "Come, You Faithful, Raise the Strain," in *Lift Up Your Hearts*, #199.

9. Charles Wesley, "Christ the Lord Is Risen Today," in *Lift Up Your Hearts*, #182.

10. New Presidents' School is a training program sponsored by the Association of Theological Schools.

11. Warren Buffett, "My Philanthropic Pledge," The Giving Pledge (website), https://givingpledge.org/pledger?pledgerId=177.

12. Christina Karns, "Why a Grateful Brain Is a Giving One," *Greater Good Magazine*, Mind & Body, December 19, 2017, https://greatergood.berkeley.edu/article/item/why_a_grateful_brain_is_a_giving_one.

13. How remarkable that it took psychologists centuries to reach Seligman's pioneering conclusion.

14. Courtney E. Ackerman, "What Is Positive Psychology & Why Is It Important?," Positive Psychology (website), April 20, 2018, https://positivepsychology.com/what-is-positive-psychology-definition.

15. Charlotte vanOyen-Witvliet, Fallon J. Richie, Lindsey M. Root Luna, and Daryl R. Van Tongeren, "Gratitude Predicts Hope and Happiness: A Two-Study Assessment of Traits and States," *Journal of Positive Psychology* 14, no. 3 (2019): 271–82; Charlotte vanOyen-Witvliet, Sung Joon Jang, Byron R. Johnson, C. Stephen Evans, Jack W. Berry, Andrew Torrance, Robert C. Roberts, John R. Peteet, Joseph Leman, and Matt Bradshaw, "Transcendent Accountability: Construct and Measurement of a Virtue That Connects Religion, Spirituality, and Positive Psychology," *Journal of Positive Psychology*, February 26, 2023, https://doi.org/10.1080/17439760.2023.2170824.

16. Patti Neighmond, "Gratitude Is Good for the Soul and Helps the Heart Too," NPR, November 23, 2015, https://www.npr.org/sections/health-shots/2015/11/23/456656055/gratitude-is-good-for-the-soul-and-it-helps-the-heart-too.

17. Neighmond, "Gratitude Is Good."

18. Quoted in Neighmond, "Gratitude Is Good."

19. D. B. Newman, A. M. Gordon, and W. B. Mendes, "Comparing Daily Physiological and Psychological Benefits of Gratitude and Optimism Using a Digital Platform," *Emotion* 21, no. 7 (2021): 1357–65, https://doi.org/10.1037/emo0001025.

20. Summer Allen, "The Science of Gratitude," white paper, John Templeton Foundation, Greater Good Science Center, May 2018, https://ggsc.berkeley.edu/images/uploads/GGSC-JTF_White_Paper-Gratitude-FINAL.pdf.

21. Scott Barry Kaufman, "Which Character Strengths Are Most Predictive of Well-Being?," *Scientific American*, August 2, 2015, https://blogs.scientificamerican.com/beautiful-minds/which-character-strengths-are-most-predictive-of-well-being.

22. Kaufman, "Which Character Strengths Are Most Predictive."

23. *Book of Common Prayer*, "The Lord's Supper or Holy Communion," https://www.churchofengland.org/prayer-and-worship/worship-texts-and-resources/book-common-prayer/lords-supper-or-holy-communion.

24. Barbara Ehrenreich, "The Selfish Side of Gratitude," *New York Times*, December 31, 2015, https://www.nytimes.com/2016/01/03/opinion/sunday/the-selfish-side-of-gratitude.html.

25. Ehrenreich, "Selfish Side of Gratitude."

Chapter 5 Biblical Themes

1. What follows is a paraphrase and quotation of Charles Kuralt, "The Dentist," in *A Life on the Road* (New York: Ballantine, 1990), 299–321, available at https://cpb-us-e1.wpmucdn.com/sites.pc.gsu.edu/dist/6/45/files/2016/11/article-Kuralt-The-Dentist-revised-1ixiwbs.pdf.

2. Kuralt, "Dentist."

3. Foundation for a Better Life, "A Lesson We Should Never Forget," Pass It On, 2021, https://www.passiton.com/positive-good-news-columns/37-a-lesson-we-should-never-forget.

4. Psalms of praise and psalms of thanksgiving are largely indistinguishable when the subject is God's goodness in general or God's deliverance in particular.

5. I find it remarkable that Israel's historians candidly report the shameful parts of Israel's history. Their candor makes them believable.

6. When Moses confronts Aaron about the golden calf, Aaron's response is cartoonish: Look, you know how bent our people are. They demanded a god, so I took gold from them, threw it into the fire, and—of all things, imagine my surprise—out came this calf! (Exod. 32:22–24).

7. The fact that Moses won't make it to the promised land with his people gives his warning extra pathos.

8. See especially Rom. 6:1–14; 2 Cor. 5:14; Col. 2:11–15; 3:1–17.

9. C. E. B. Cranfield, *The Epistle to the Romans*, 2 vols. (Edinburgh: T&T Clark, 1975), 1:299–300.

10. Infants may be immersed too. Greek Orthodox churches do it all the time.

11. Col. 3:12–17; Eph. 4:25–5:2; 5:15–20; Gal. 5:22–23; Rom. 12:9–21. These virtues-of-Christ passages may be remembered as follows: Col. 3 plus Eph. 4 plus Gal. 5 equals Rom. 12. The scheme works both alphabetically and arithmetically.

Chapter 6 Thank God! Why?

1. This story is available online at multiple sites. I'm quoting from and paraphrasing Courtney Carver, "The Mexican Fisherman," The Simplicity Space (website), https://bemorewithless.com/the-story-of-the-mexican-fisherman.

2. Philip Yancey, *Disappointment with God: Three Questions No One Asks Aloud* (Grand Rapids: Zondervan, 2015).

3. David G. Allan, "How to Become More Grateful, and Why That Will Make You Happier, Healthier, and More Resilient," CNN, May 19, 2022, https://www .cnn.com/2022/05/19/health/gratitude-wisdom-project-chasing-life-wellness /index.html.

4. A prequel to the TV series *Yellowstone*.

5. Patricia MacLachlan, *Sarah, Plain and Tall* (New York: HarperCollins, 1985).

6. MacLachlan, *Sarah, Plain and Tall*, 17.

7. MacLachlan, *Sarah, Plain and Tall*, 14.

8. MacLachlan, *Sarah, Plain and Tall*, 23.

9. Ponder one detail: "Your wagon tracks overflow with richness." Are we invited to imagine a wagon piled so high with fruit and grain that it spills part of its load onto its own receding tracks?

10. C. S. Lewis, *Surprised by Joy: The Shape of My Early Life* (New York: Harcourt, Brace, 1955), 229. Lewis is himself the resentful convert he describes here.

Chapter 7 It Could Always Be Worse

1. The following is a paraphrase of Margot Zemach, *It Could Always Be Worse: A Yiddish Folk Tale Retold and with Pictures* (New York: Farrar, Straus & Giroux, 1976).

2. Quoted in David Steindl-Rast, introduction to *Words of Gratitude for Mind, Body, and Soul*, by Robert A. Emmons and Joanna Hill (Conshohocken, PA: Templeton, 2001), 6–7.

3. Quoted in A. J. Jacobs, *Thanks a Thousand: A Gratitude Journey from Bean to Cup* (London: TED Books, 2018), 23.

4. Jeff Chapman, "Gratitude: The Echo of Grace" (sermon, Faith Presbyterian Church, Sacramento, CA, November 26, 2006).

5. Hans Rosling, "The Magic Washing Machine," TEDWomen 2010, https://www.ted.com/talks/hans_rosling_the_magic_washing_machine.

6. Marilynne Robinson, *Gilead* (New York: Farrar, Straus & Giroux, 2004), 31.

7. Robinson, *Gilead*, 35.

8. Robert A. Emmons, *Thanks! How Practicing Gratitude Can Make You Happier* (Boston: Houghton Mifflin, 2008).

9. Emmons, *Thanks!*, 166–69.

10. Emmons, *Thanks!*, 173.

11. Emmons, *Thanks!*, 159.

12. Remarkably—and following a centuries-long Jewish tradition—Jesus prays Ps. 22:1 just before his death (Mark 15:34).

13. Glenn Packiam, "Five Things to Know about Lament," N. T. Wright Online (website), https://www.ntwrightonline.org/five-things-to-know-about-lament.

14. Mark 14:55, 44, 37, 56, 66–72.

Chapter 8 Savoring and Celebrating

1. A. J. Jacobs, *Thanks a Thousand: A Gratitude Journey from Bean to Cup* (London: TED, 2015).

2. Jacobs, *Thanks a Thousand*, 76.

3. Jacobs, *Thanks a Thousand*, 78–82.

4. Solomon Schimmel, "Gratitude in Judaism," in *The Psychology of Gratitude*, ed. Robert A. Emmons and Michael E. McCullough (Oxford: Oxford University Press, 2004), 42.

5. Schimmel, "Gratitude in Judaism," 43.

6. Wikipedia, s.v. "Happy Birthday to You," last updated April 24, 2023, https://en.wikipedia.org/wiki/Happy_Birthday_to_You.

7. Wikipedia, s.v. "Las Mañanitas," last updated December 15, 2022, https://en.wikipedia.org/wiki/Las_Mañanitas.

8. Such secular offerings as "Jingle Bells" and "Rudolph, the Red-Nosed Reindeer" are generally termed Christmas songs, not Christmas carols.

9. "518th Birthday of the First Common Language Hymnal," Missions Box (website), January 16, 2019, https://missionsbox.org/news/january-1501-1st-common-language-hymnal.

10. *Lift Up Your Hearts: Psalms, Hymns, and Spiritual Songs* (Grand Rapids: Faith Alive, 2013). Pentecost celebrates an outpouring of the Holy Spirit but may be counted as an event of Christ too: Jesus had promised his followers that he would send them "another Advocate" (John 14:16), a promise fulfilled at Pentecost.

Chapter 9 Taking Care

1. Fred Gipson, *Old Yeller* (New York: HarperCollins, 1956), 60.

2. Robert C. Roberts, *Taking the Word to Heart: Self and Other in an Age of Therapies* (Grand Rapids: Eerdmans, 1993), 205–19.

3. Roberts, *Taking the Word*, 209.

4. This model duplicates Jesus's words in Mark 10:8.

5. Roberts, *Taking the Word*, 216–17.

6. Heidelberg Catechism, answers 86 and 90 (emphasis added), in *Ecumenical Creeds and Reformed Confessions* (Grand Rapids: Faith Alive, 1988), 54.

7. See Jonathan Edwards, *The Religious Affections* (Edinburgh: Banner of Truth, 1986).

8. Edwards, *Religious Affections*, 308.

9. Edwards, *Religious Affections*, 348 (emphasis added).

10. John Calvin, *Institutes of the Christian Religion* 2.7.12, ed. John T. McNeill, trans. Ford Lewis Battles, 2 vols. (Philadelphia: Westminster, 1960), 1:360.

11. A verse of devastating grace: "God proves his love for us in that while we still were sinners Christ died for us" (Rom. 5:8).

Chapter 10 A Cornucopia of Gifts

1. Defense POW/MIA Accounting Agency, "Soldier Accounted for from World War II (Hofman, D.)," news release, August 31, 2022, https://www.dpaa.mil/News -Stories/News-Releases/PressReleaseArticleView/Article/3098273/soldier-ac counted-for-from-world-war-ii-hofman-d.

2. Multiple intelligences create the "blessed web of dependence" required to put a cup of good coffee on our table. We saw this in chap. 8.

3. The main source for what follows is "What We Do," Doctors Without Borders, https://www.doctorswithoutborders.org/what-we-do.

4. Westminster Shorter Catechism, 1647, answer 1, available at https://www .apuritansmind.com/westminster-standards/shorter-catechism.

Notes to Sidebars

Chapter 1

a. Charles M. Schulz, *Gobble Up, Snoopy!* (New York: Simon Spotlight, 2019).

b. Frank Darabont, *The Shawshank Redemption: The Shooting Script*, introduction by Stephen King (New York: Newmarket, 1996), 61–62.

c. *Book of Common Prayer*, "The Lord's Supper or Holy Communion," https://www.churchofengland.org/prayer-and-worship/worship-texts-and-resources/book-common-prayer/lords-supper-or-holy-communion.

Chapter 2

a. G. K. Chesterton, *Orthodoxy* (Garden City, NY: Image Books, 1959), 60.

b. C. S. Lewis, *Letters to Malcolm: Chiefly on Prayer* (San Francisco: HarperOne, 2017), 122.

Chapter 3

a. For an exploration of how uneasily grace lives inside an ethos of capitalism, see Scott Hoezee, *The Riddle of Grace: Applying Grace to the Christian Life* (Grand Rapids: Eerdmans, 1996), 83–123.

b. Thomas L. Friedman, "All Fall Down," *New York Times*, October 26, 2008, https://www.nytimes.com/2008/11/26/opinion/26iht-edfriedman.1.18173018.html.

c. In the Bible's wisdom literature, a sluggard is a fool. In this case, framed up almost as a cartoon, he's a fool not only for not planting anything but also for then looking at harvest time to see what has come up.

Chapter 4

a. John Claypool, "Life Is a Gift," in *A Chorus of Witnesses: Model Sermons for Today's Preacher*, ed. Thomas G. Long and Cornelius Plantinga Jr. (Grand Rapids: Eerdmans, 1994), 125.

b. Drawing from Brent Fulton, "Chinese Christians Deserve a Better Label Than 'Persecuted,'" *Christianity Today*, October 9, 2020, https://www.christianitytoday.com/ct/2020/october-web-only/chinese-christians-persecuted-narrative-church-xi-jinping.html.

Chapter 5

a. Danielle Slutsky and Misha Slutsky, "Dayenu with English, Hebrew, and Transliteration," Haggadot.com, https://www.haggadot.com/clip/dayenu-english-hebrew-and-transliteration.

Chapter 6

a. Walt Whitman, *Specimen Days and Collect* (1882; repr., North Chelmsford, MA: Courier Corporation, 1995), 150.

b. The Canons of Dort, Third/Fourth Point, articles 11, 12, in *Ecumenical Creeds and Reformed Confessions* (Grand Rapids: Faith Alive, 1988), 134–35.

Chapter 7

a. Matthew Henry, quoted in Nancy Leigh DeMoss, with Lawrence Kimbrough, *Choosing Gratitude: Your Journey to Joy* (Chicago: Moody, 2009), 62.

b. Alphonse Karr, *Lettres écrites de mon jardin* (Letters written from my garden) (Paris: Michel Lévy Frères, 1853), 293. Karr attributes the saying to an anonymous source.

Chapter 8

a. Barbara Kingsolver, *Animal, Vegetable, Miracle: A Year of Food Life* (New York: Harper, 2007), 287.

Chapter 9

a. Anatole France, quoted in Billy Holland, "Until One Has Loved an Animal," *Jackson Sun*, December 6, 2019, https://www.jacksonsun.com/story/news/2019/12/06/until-one-has-loved-animal/4352308002.

b. A friend of mine who wishes to remain anonymous.

c. This quotation is widely attributed to David Lee Roth.

Chapter 10

a. Nate Rawlings, "The Warrior Ethos: Why We Leave No One Behind," *Time*, May 17, 2012, https://nation.time.com/2012/05/17/the-warrior-ethos-why-we-leave-no-one-behind.

b. Kim Ann Zimmerman, "Great Facts about the Five Great Lakes," Live Science, June 29, 2017, https://www.livescience.com/29312-great-lakes.html.